Voicing Modes

A chord-voicing approach to hearing and practicing modes.
For comping, improvisation, reharmonization & composition.

By Noel Johnston

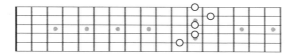

Front cover and other image credits: Adobe Stock images and Noel Johnston
Constellation: Cassiopeia
Chord shape: (All-purpose F Melodic Minor voicing) A♭Maj7#5#11 but works with various other
roots in F Melodic Minor; E7alt, B♭7#11, etc. (and it also works over C Harmonic-Major)

Contents

Fundamental sound surrounded by its related sounds

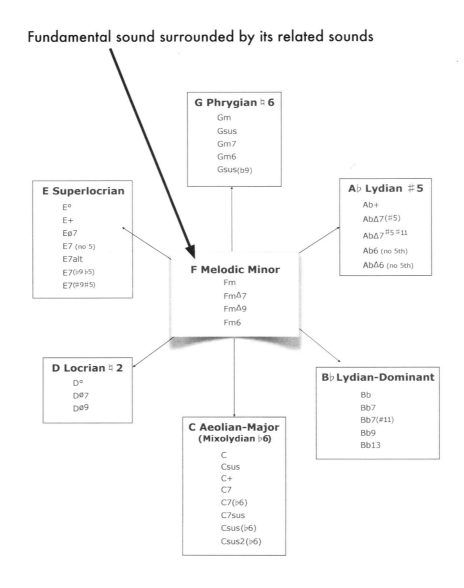

G Phrygian ♮6
Gm
Gsus
Gm7
Gm6
Gsus(b9)

E Superlocrian
E°
E+
Eø7
E7 (no 5)
E7alt
E7(b9 b5)
E7(#9#5)

A♭ Lydian ♯5
Ab+
AbΔ7(#5)
AbΔ7 #5 #11
Ab6 (no 5th)
AbΔ6 (no 5th)

F Melodic Minor
Fm
FmΔ7
FmΔ9
Fm6

D Locrian ♮2
D°
Dø7
Dø9

B♭ Lydian-Dominant
Bb
Bb7
Bb7(#11)
Bb9
Bb13

C Aeolian-Major
(Mixolydian b6)
C
Csus
C+
C7
C7(b6)
C7sus
Csus(b6)
Csus2(b6)

How to interpret the mode/chord boxes:

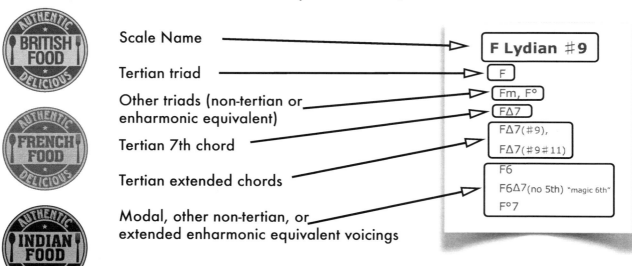

Scale Name — **F Lydian ♯9**

Tertian triad — F

Other triads (non-tertian or enharmonic equivalent) — Fm, F°

Tertian 7th chord — FΔ7

Tertian extended chords — FΔ7(♯9), FΔ7(♯9♯11)

Modal, other non-tertian, or extended enharmonic equivalent voicings — F6, F6Δ7(no 5th) "magic 6th", F°7

Introduction.

Modes are often at first understood in relation to a parent scale. While this can be helpful as a starting point and for developing muscle memory, in practice it doesn't always point the player to the right chord tones in relation to the sound. In other words, it doesn't help make the changes.

To use modes to make the changes, one must be able to relate the scale shape to a chord voicing - a chord voicing that outlines the essential few tones in a sea of seven notes. These voicings can vary depending on the amount of color desired. The color desired is dependent on musical style/genre, and whether or not the chord is functional in a progression or static in its modality. These essential tones are not always 1,3,5,7 (tertian harmony - stacked in 3rds).

While most chords in jazz and improv-based music are expressed in one of four tertian-voicing archetypes (Major, Minor, Dominant, or Diminished) — this is a false tetrachotomy. There are more than four.

To capture some other sounds that many composers intend, especially in compositions written in the last 50 years (and in Classical music, 150 years) one must add a few other archetypes. While those indicated in this book are not exhaustive, they will open your ears to other ways of expressing harmony while still staying true to the key center.

While exploring other ways to voice the modes, keep in mind that these are not just for comping and soloing. Feel free to use them as a starting point for composition and reharmonization. The use of "pivot voicings" instead of just pivot chords can open up your understanding of harmonic relationships in multiple ways.

Enjoy exploring.

-Noel

P. S. This book is way more fun if you use a looper pedal.

Now go eat before you turn the page...

Triads and basic 7th chords

- Everything on the plate is nutritionally "functional"
- Flavoring/spices/sauce is mostly unimportant
- The 'staple' is the essence of the dish.

- Every note is functional - each note has harmonic purpose & direction.
- Harmonic gravity (tension/resolution tendencies)
- 3rds (maybe 5ths) & 7ths make up the essence of the sound

Extended chords
& idiomatic Jazz voicings

- While the protein & starch ("functional" food) may make up the foundation of the the dish, the flavoring/spices/sauce is also essential to the recipe.
- The 'staples' with the extra stuff on top make up the essence of the dish.

- Notes in the lower register are functional
- Harmonic gravity (tension/resolution tendency) is somewhat important
- The addition of one or more upper extensions (color tones, flavor notes) such as 9th, 11th, 13th, #11 are essential.

Modal Voicings

- The recipe starts with the spices.
- Flavoring/spices/sauce is the foundation.
- The choice or omission of a 'staple' is irrelevant to the essence of the dish.

- Every voicing note is for flavor.
- Hidden or no harmonic gravity, can vamp or stay on one sound.
- Non-functional - does not obey tension/resolution tendencies.
- 3rd & 7th not necessary because upper extensions/color tones make up the essence of the sound.

Some different VOICING ARCHETYPES and their essence (fundamental characteristics)

Functional:	
Major:	3rd, 7th
Minor:	♭3rd, 5th
Dominant:	3rd, ♭7th
Diminished:	♭3rd, ♭5th

Non-Functional:	
Sus:	2nd, 5th / 4th, 5th
Phrygian:	♭2nd, 4th
Aeolian:	2nd, ♭6th

What's in a name?

Some scales can have more than one name, but differences in name can evoke different properties. In other words, a name can hint at a certain way to voice a sound. One may be more interesting/useful than the other depending on the context. Take these examples:

□Example 1
5th-mode Melodic Minor. Interval structure: W-W-1/2-W-1/2-W-W (1, 2, 3, 4, 5, ♭6, ♭7).
It can be voiced and named these two ways:

Mixolydian ♭6 -- evokes a Dominant voicing: 1, 3, 5, ♭7 with a ♭13 ("French food" voicing)
Aeolian-Major -- evokes a non-functional, Aeolian voicing: 1, 2, 5, ♭6 but with a major 3rd ("Indian food" voicing)

□Example 2
2nd-mode Melodic Minor. Interval structure: 1/2-W-W-W-W-1/2-W (1, ♭2, ♭3, 4, 5, 6, ♭7).
It can be voiced and named these two ways:

Dorian ♭2 -- evokes a minor voicing: 1, ♭3, 5, ♭7 with a ♭2 ("French food" voicing)
Phrygian ♮6 -- evokes a non-functional, Phrygian voicing: 1, ♭2, 4, 5 but with a ♮6 ("Indian food" voicing)

Phrygian

•Phrygian, the 3rd mode of the major scale, has the interval structure:
1/2 - W - W - W - 1/2 - W - W (1 - ♭2 - ♭3 - 4 - 5 - ♭6 - ♭7)

•Phrygian can be voiced functionally or modally.

•When voiced in 3rds (tertian harmony), it spells a minor triad, or a minor-7th chord. Extended tertian chords in this mode are not common.

•Functionally, A iii can substitude for a I chord (1st inversion I chords are not true iii chords), and iii chords in a progression are often changed to be secondary dominants - altered (raised 3rd) to give stronger harmonic gravity to the vi; When resolving from iii to vi the 3rd is often raised (making a leading tone to the root of vi) making a III → vi progression. Phrygian with a ♮3 is known as "Phrygian-Dominant" or "Spanish Phrygian."

•With traditional tertian chord nomenclature, the MODAL Phrygian sound can be written in a variety of ways such as Fm triad ↔ Gm over G bass (cadence or triad pair over a static bass note), or these slash chords or change-bass chords:
    A♭△7♯11/G, Fm6/G, B♭13/G, or D⌀7/G.
    See Wayne Shorter's "Witch Hunt" (Last 4 bars), and John Coltrane's "Naima" (bridge)

•MODAL Phrygian can be thought of as an "indian food" voicing... Where the bass note is the actual root of the sound, and *without the 3rd or 7th* which are non-essential in Phrygian. (Also, without the ♭6 - an essential Aeolian tone - because it threatens to sound more like a 1st inversion I chord than a true Phrygian)
If we assign 1, ♭2, 4, 5 as the essential tones, **Gsus(♭2)** expresses that interval structure - leaving open the potential for many more types of "Phrygian" will the addition of different types of 3rds, 6ths, & 7ths.

•The following pages contain some different types of Phrygian (& their relatives) and also some shapes for voicing the essence of modal Phrygian. As you will see, multiple possibilities can result from assigning 1, ♭2, 4, 5 as the essential tones.

"Essential Phrygian" - made up of 1, ♭2, 4, 5

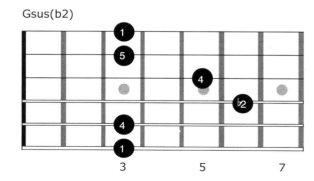

Nerdy Phrygian trivia:
•Phrygian (3rd-major scale) in retrograde is a Major Scale (makes major keys a 3rd away actually 'related')
•Phrygian-Dominant in retrograde is a Harmonic Major Scale.
•Phrygian ♮6 in retrograde is a Melodic Minor scale.

Essential Phrygian
Gsus(♭9)

"Essence" of non-functional Phrygian: **1, ♭2, ♮4, ♮5**.

(These notes would make up the SHELL VOICING and the basic arpeggio)

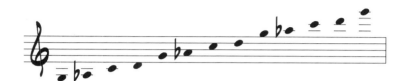

The non-essential tones are: ♭**3 or** ♮**3**

(these notes are the color tones or upper extensions)   ♭**6 or** ♮**6**

♭**7 or** ♮**7**

With those variables, there are 8 possible combinations:

♭3 ♭6 ♭7 *

♮3 ♭6 ♭7 *

♭3 ♮6 ♭7 *

♭3 ♭6 ♮7

♮3 ♭6 ♮7 *

♮3 ♮6 ♭7 *

♭3 ♮6 ♮7

♮3 ♮6 ♮7

(* indicates sounds that are less obscure and more 'useful' than the others)

Here are 5 *useful* sounds that fit this Phrygian voicing:

1, ♭2, ♭**3**, ♮4, ♮5, ♭6, ♭**7** (Basic Phrygian - 3rd mode of the major scale)

1, ♭2, ♮**3**, ♮4, ♮5, ♭6, ♭**7** (Phrygian-Dom./Spanish Phryg. - 5th mode Harmonic Minor)

1, ♭2, ♭**3**, ♮4, ♮5, ♮**6**, ♭**7** (Phrygian ♮6 - 2nd mode Melodic Minor)

1, ♭2, ♮**3**, ♮4, ♮5, ♭**6**, ♮**7** (Double Harmonic Maj - 5th mode Hungarian min or Double harmonic min)

1, ♭2, ♮**3**, ♮4, ♮5, ♮**6**, ♭**7** (Phrygian-Dom (♮6) - 5th mode of Harmonic Major)

iii. G Phrygian

Ab Lydian
Ab, Ab2
AbΔ7, AbΔ9
AbΔ7(#11)
Ab6
AbΔ6

F Dorian
Fm
Fsus
Fm7, Fm9
Fm11
Fm6

G Phrygian
Gm
Gsus
Gm7
Gsus(b9)

Bb Mixolydian
Bb, Bb2, Bbsus
Bb7
Bb9, Bb13
Bb7sus
Bb9sus
Bb13sus

Eb Major (Ionian)
Eb, Eb2, Ebsus
EbΔ7
EbΔ9
Eb6

D Locrian
D°
Dø7

C Aeolian
Cm
Csus
Cm7
Cm9
Csus2(b6)

V. G Phrygian-Dominant

Ab Lydian #9
Ab
Abm, Ab°
AbΔ7
AbΔ7(#9)
AbΔ7(#9#11)
Ab6
Ab6Δ7 "magic 6th"
Ab°7

F Dorian #4
Fm
F°
Fm7
Fø7
F°7

G Phrygian-Dominant
G
G+
G7
G7(b9)
Gsus(b9) "phrygian"

B Superlocrian bb7
B°
B+
B°7
B6 (no 5th)

Eb Ionian #5
Eb+
EbΔ7(#5)
Eb6 (no 5th)
Eb6Δ7 "magic 6th"

D Locrian ♮6
D°
Dø7
D°7

C Harmonic Minor
Cm
CmΔ7
CmΔ9
Csus2(b6) "aeolian"

ii. G Phrygian ♮6

Ab Lydian #5
Ab+
AbΔ7(#5)
AbΔ7 #5 #11
Ab6 (no 5th)
AbΔ6 (no 5th)

F Melodic Minor
Fm
FmΔ7
FmΔ9
Fm6

G Phrygian ♮6
Gm
Gsus
Gm7
Gm6
Gsus(b9)

Bb Lydian-Dominant
Bb
Bb7
Bb7(#11)
Bb9
Bb13

E Superlocrian
E°
E+
Eø7
E7 (no 5)
E7alt
E7(b9 b5)
E7(#9#5)

D Locrian ♮2
D°
Dø7
Dø9

C Aeolian-Major (Mixolydian b6)
C
Csus
C+
C7
C7(b6)
C7sus
Csus(b6)
Csus2(b6)

I. G Double Harmonic Major
(5th mode Hungarian Minor)

Ab Lydian #9#6
Ab
Abm, F°
AbΔ7, AbΔ7(#9), AbΔ7(#11)
Ab7, Ab7(#9), Ab7(#11)
AbmΔ7, Abm7
Abm7b5, Ab°Δ7
Ab7(Δ7)

F# Locrian bb3bb7
F#sus2b5 ("bb3")
F#°bb3 (G#7/F#)
F#sus2b6(b5) (D7b5/F#)
F#susb6b2 (G/F#)

G Dbl-Harm Major
G
G+, Gsus
GΔ7
GΔ7#5
GΔ7(b6) "Herbie"
Gsus(b9) "Phrygian"
Gsus(b6)

B Ultralocrian ♮5
(Phrygian b4 bb7)
Bm
B, B+
Bm6
B6
B°7(b6/#5)

Eb Ionian #5 #2
Eb+
EbΔ7(#5)
EbΔ7(#9#5)
Eb6 (no 5th)
EbΔ6 (no 5) "Magic 6"
Ebsus(b6)(no 5)
Eb°7(b6/#5)

D Mixolydian b5b9
D(b5)
D7 (no 5)
D7(b5), B7(b9 b5)
D6 (no 5th)
D13 (no 5)
D13(b9)

C Dbl-Harm Minor
Cm
C°
CmΔ7, CmΔ9
C°Δ7
Csus2(b6) "Aeolian"

8

V. G Mixolydian ♭2

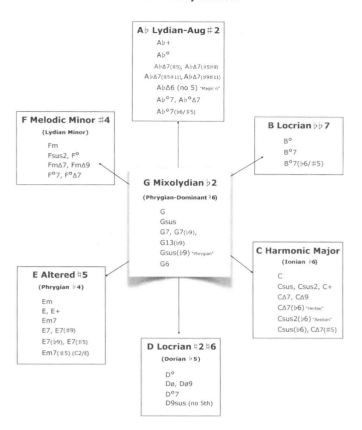

F Melodic Minor ♯4
(Lydian Minor)

Fm
Fsus2, F°
Fm△7, Fm△9
F°7, F°△7

A♭ Lydian-Aug ♯2

A♭+
A♭°
A♭△7(♯5), A♭△7(♯5♯9)
A♭△7(♯5♯11), A♭△7(♯9♯11)
A♭△6 (no 5) "Magic 6"
A♭°7, A♭°△7
A♭°7(♭6/♯5)

B Locrian ♭♭7

B°
B°7
B°7(♭6/♯5)

G Mixolydian ♭2
(Phrygian-Dominant ♮6)

G
Gsus
G7, G7(♭9),
G13(♭9)
Gsus(♭9) "Phrygian"
G6

C Harmonic Major
(Ionian ♭6)

C
Csus, Csus2, C+
C△7, C△9
C△7(♭6) "Herbie"
Csus2(♭6) "Aeolian"
Csus(♭6), C△7(♯5)

E Altered ♮5
(Phrygian ♭4)

Em
E, E+
Em7
E7, E7(♯9)
E7(♭9), E7(♯5)
Em7(♯5) (C2/E)

D Locrian ♯2 ♮6
(Dorian ♭5)

D°
Dø, Dø9
D°7
D9sus (no 5th)

Larger size modal relative diagrams are in the reference section of this book starting pg. 72.

For interactive modal relative diagrams, download the "Voicing Modes" iOS app, or "Voicing Modes" web app at www.noeljohnston.com

Gsus(b2)

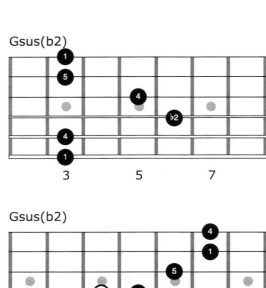

Gsus(b2)

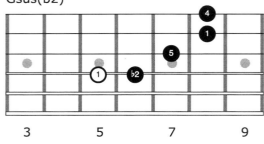

Gsus(b2)

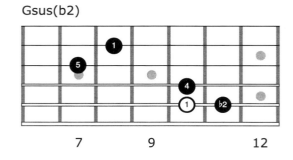

Gsus(b2)

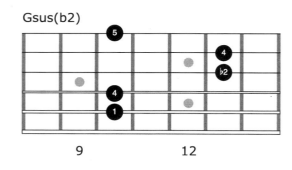

Gsus(b2)

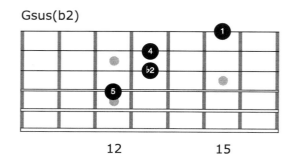

G Phrygian arpeggio Position 1

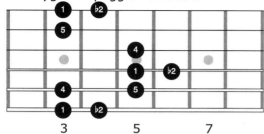

G Phrygian arpeggio Position 2

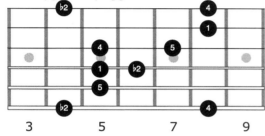

G Phrygian arpeggio Position 3

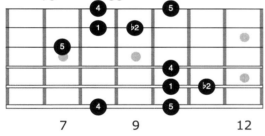

G Phrygian arpeggio Position 4

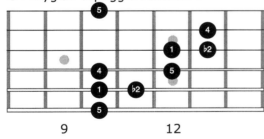

G Phrygian arpeggio Position 5

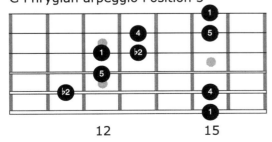

G Phrygian arpeggio Position 1

G Phrygian arpeggio Position 2

G Phrygian arpeggio Position 3

G Phrygian arpeggio Position 4

G Phrygian arpeggio Position 5

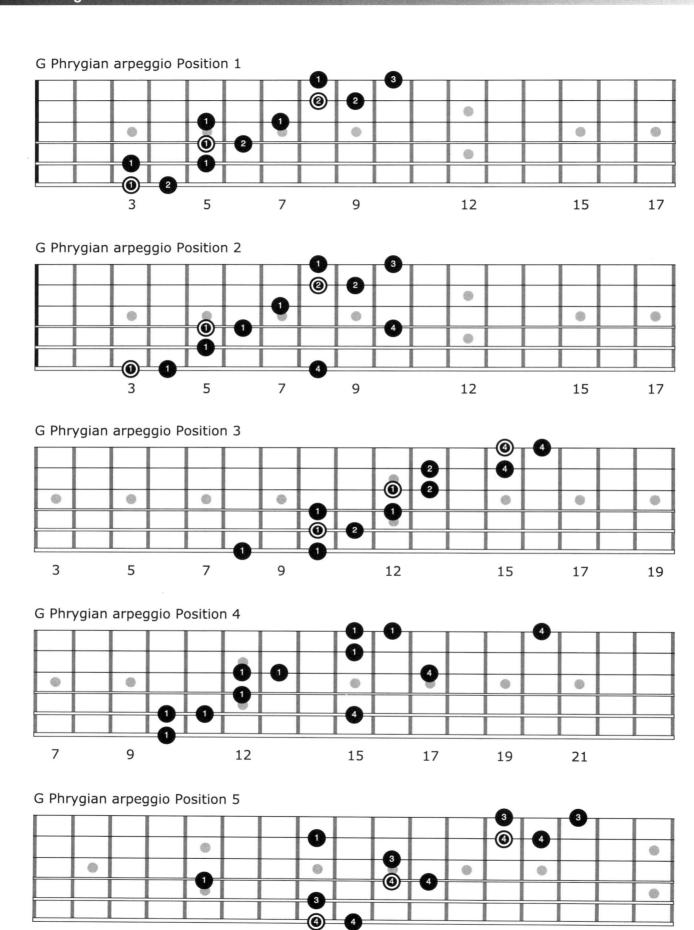

- This one uses mostly Phrygian voicings.
- Keys used: A Phrygian (F Major), A Phrygian ♮6 (G Melodic Minor), A Phrygian-Dominant (D Harmonic Minor)
- Measures 9-12 should be thought of as F Phrygian-Dominant ♮6 (Bb Harmonic Major).

Phrygian Etude #1

Noel Johnston

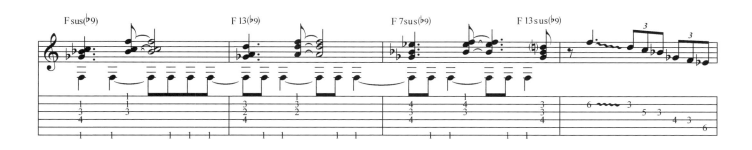

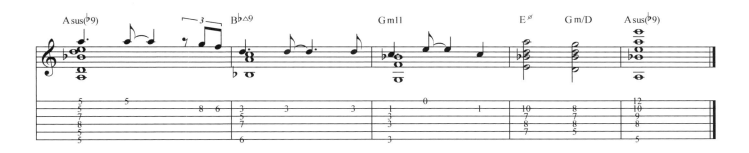

- This one uses the "essence" of G-Phrygian (1, b2, 4, 5) as the only common thread throughout the various key centers used.
- It uses chords from Eb Major (G Phrygian), F Melodic Minor (G Phrygian ♮6), and C Harmonic Minor (G Phrygian-Dominant).
- This one can be played chord-melody style (rubato or in time).
- Also, try recording the changes in a looper and hear how G-phrygian arpeggios will sound through the changes.

Phrygian Etude #2

Noel Johnston

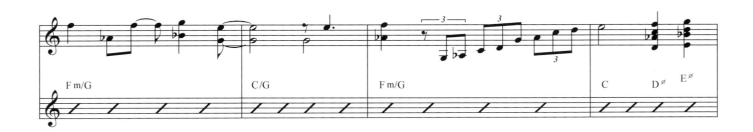

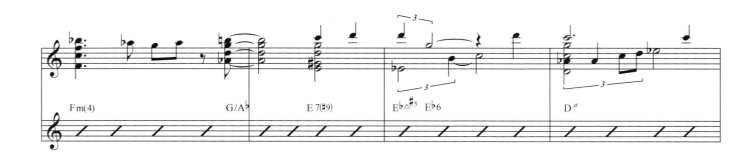

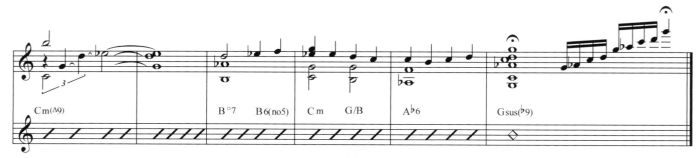

For performance examples: https://www.youtube.com/user/nohjoh08

Aeolian

•Aeolian can be voiced as a functional or modal voicing, and it is very common as a functional minor chord, however...

•The following pages contain a suggested voicing for MODAL Aeolian and the multiple possibilities that can result from assigning 1, 2, 5, ♭6 as the essential tones.

•"Essential Aeolian" voicing (1, 2, 5, ♭6)

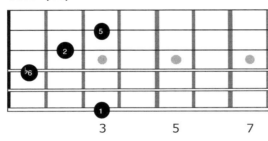

•This "Essential Aeolian" voicing (1, 2, 5, ♭6) has the same interval structure as the "Essential Phrygian" voicing (1, ♭2, 4, 5) but with a different root. You may think of it as an inversion of Phrygian, but it resonates differently.

Nerdy Aeolian trivia:

•Aeolian (6th mode Major scale) in retrograde is a Mixolydian scale.
•Harmonic Minor in retrograde is Phrygian-Dominant 6
•Aeolian-Major in retrograde is the SAME (Aeolian-Major).

Essential Aeolian

Gsus2(♭6)

"Essence" of non-functional Aeolian: **1, ♮2, ♮5, ♭6**.

(These notes would make up the SHELL VOICING and the basic arpeggio)

The non-essential tones are:

(these notes are the color tones or upper extensions)

♭3 or ♮3

♮4 or ♯4

♭7 or ♮7

With those variables, there are 8 possible combinations:

♭3 ♮4 ♭7 *

♮3 ♮4 ♭7 *

♭3 ♯4 ♭7

♭3 ♮4 ♮7 *

♮3 ♮4 ♮7 *

♮3 ♯4 ♭7

♭3 ♯4 ♮7 *

♮3 ♯4 ♮7

(* indicates sounds that are less obscure and more 'useful' than the others)

Here are 5 *useful* sounds that fit this Aeolian voicing:

1, ♮2, ♭**3**, ♮**4**, ♮**5**, ♭6, ♭**7** (Basic Aeolian - 6th mode of the major scale)

1, ♮2, ♮**3**, ♮**4**, ♮**5**, ♭6, ♭**7** (Aeolian Major/Mixolydian b6 - 5th mode Melodic Minor)

1, ♮2, ♭**3**, ♮**4**, ♮**5**, ♭6, ♮**7** (Harmonic Minor)

1, ♮2, ♮**3**, ♮**4**, ♮**5**, ♭6, ♮**7** (Harmonic Major)

1, ♮2, ♭**3**, ♯**4**, ♮**5**, ♭6, ♮**7** (Hungarian Minor, aka Double Harmonic Minor)

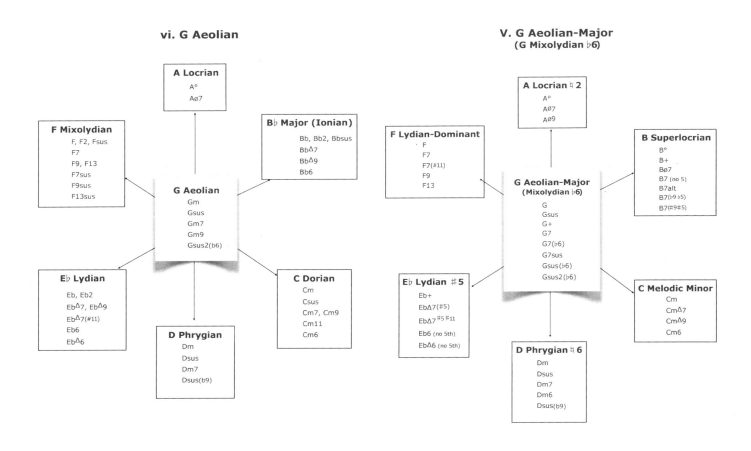

vi. G Aeolian

A Locrian
- A°
- Aø7

F Mixolydian
- F, F2, Fsus
- F7
- F9, F13
- F7sus
- F9sus
- F13sus

Bb Major (Ionian)
- Bb, Bb2, Bbsus
- BbΔ7
- BbΔ9
- Bb6

G Aeolian
- Gm
- Gsus
- Gm7
- Gm9
- Gsus2(b6)

Eb Lydian
- Eb, Eb2
- EbΔ7, EbΔ9
- EbΔ7(#11)
- Eb6
- EbΔ6

D Phrygian
- Dm
- Dsus
- Dm7
- Dsus(b9)

C Dorian
- Cm
- Csus
- Cm7, Cm9
- Cm11
- Cm6

V. G Aeolian-Major
(G Mixolydian b6)

A Locrian ♮2
- A°
- Aø7
- Aø9

F Lydian-Dominant
- F
- F7
- F7(#11)
- F9
- F13

B Superlocrian
- B°
- B+
- Bø7
- B7 (no 5)
- B7alt
- B7(b9 b5)
- B7(#9#5)

G Aeolian-Major
(Mixolydian b6)
- G
- Gsus
- G+
- G7
- G7(b6)
- G7sus
- Gsus(b6)
- Gsus2(b6)

Eb Lydian #5
- Eb+
- EbΔ7(#5)
- EbΔ7 #5 #11
- Eb6 (no 5th)
- EbΔ6 (no 5th)

C Melodic Minor
- Cm
- CmΔ7
- CmΔ9
- Cm6

D Phrygian ♮6
- Dm
- Dsus
- Dm7
- Dm6
- Dsus(b9)

i. G Harmonic Minor

A Locrian ♮6
- A°
- Aø7
- A°7

F# Superlocrian bb7
- F#°
- F#+
- F#°7
- F#6 (no 5th)

Bb Ionian #5
- Bb+
- BbΔ7(#5)
- Bb6 (no 5th)
- Bb6Δ7 "magic 6th"

G Harmonic Minor
- Gm
- GmΔ7
- GmΔ9
- Gsus2(b6) "aeolian"

Eb Lydian #9
- Eb
- Ebm, Eb°
- EbΔ7
- EbΔ7(#9)
- EbΔ7(#9#11)
- Eb6
- Eb6Δ7 "magic 6th"
- Eb°7

D Phrygian-Dominant
- D
- D+
- D7
- D7(b9)
- Dsus(b9) "phrygian"

C Dorian #4
- Cm
- C°
- Cm7
- Cø7
- C°7

I. G Harmonic Major

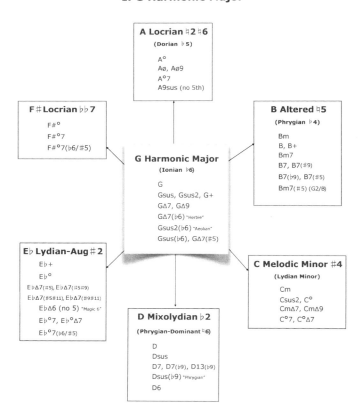

A Locrian ♮2 ♮6
(Dorian b5)
- A°
- Aø, Aø9
- A°7
- A9sus (no 5th)

F# Locrian bb7
- F#°
- F#°7
- F#°7(b6/#5)

B Altered ♮5
(Phrygian b4)
- Bm
- B, B+
- Bm7
- B7, B7(#9)
- B7(b9), B7(#5)
- Bm7(#5) (G2/B)

G Harmonic Major
(Ionian b6)
- G
- Gsus, Gsus2, G+
- GΔ7, GΔ9
- GΔ7(b6) "Herbie"
- Gsus2(b6) "Aeolian"
- Gsus(b6), GΔ7(#5)

Eb Lydian-Aug #2
- Eb+
- Eb°
- EbΔ7(#5), EbΔ7(#5#9)
- EbΔ7(#5#11), EbΔ7(#9#11)
- EbΔ6 (no 5) "Magic 6"
- EbΔ7, Eb°Δ7
- Eb°7(b6/#5)

D Mixolydian b2
(Phrygian-Dominant ♮6)
- D
- Dsus
- D7, D7(b9), D13(b9)
- Dsus(b9) "Phrygian"
- D6

C Melodic Minor #4
(Lydian Minor)
- Cm
- Csus2, C°
- CmΔ7, CmΔ9
- C°7, C°Δ7

i. G Double Harmonic Minor
(Hungarian Minor, Harmonic Minor #4)

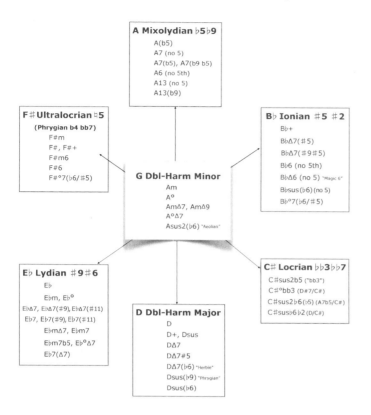

A Mixolydian ♭5♭9
A(b5)
A7 (no 5)
A7(b5), A7(b9 b5)
A6 (no 5th)
A13 (no 5)
A13(b9)

F♯Ultralocrian ♮5
(Phrygian b4 bb7)
F#m
F#, F#+
F#m6
F#6
F#°7(b6/#5)

B♭ Ionian ♯5 ♯2
Bb+
BbΔ7(#5)
BbΔ7(#9#5)
Bb6 (no 5th)
BbΔ6 (no 5) "Magic 6"
Bbsus(b6)(no 5)
Bb°7(b6/#5)

G Dbl-Harm Minor
Am
A°
AmΔ7, AmΔ9
A°Δ7
Asus2(b6) "Aeolian"

E♭ Lydian ♯9♯6
Eb
Ebm, Eb°
EbΔ7, EbΔ7(#9), EbΔ7(#11)
Eb7, Eb7(#9), Eb7(#11)
EbmΔ7, Ebm7
Ebm7b5, Eb°Δ7
Eb7(Δ7)

D Dbl-Harm Major
D
D+, Dsus
DΔ7
DΔ7#5
DΔ7(b6) "Herbie"
Dsus(b9) "Phrygian"
Dsus(b6)

C♯ Locrian ♭♭3♭♭7
C#sus2b5 ("bb3")
C#°bb3 (D#7/C#)
C#sus2b6(b5) (A7b5/C#)
C#susb6b2 (D/C#)

Larger size modal relative diagrams are in the reference section of this book starting pg. 72.

For interactive modal relative diagrams, download the "Voicing Modes" iOS app, or "Voicing Modes" web app at www.noeljohnston.com

Gsus2(b6)

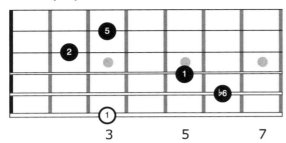

Gsus2(b6)

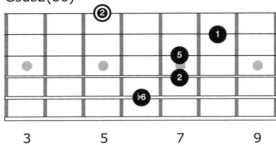

Gsus2(b6)

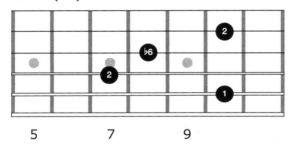

Gsus2(b6)

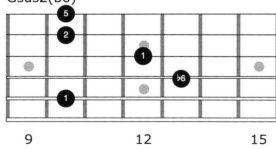

Gsus2(b6)

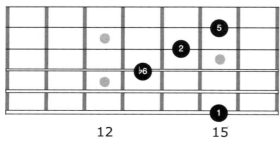

G Aeolian arpeggio Position 1

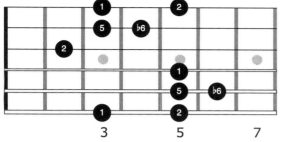

G Aeolian arpeggio Position 2

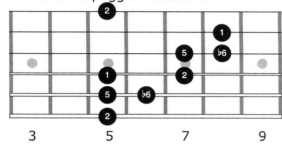

G Aeolian arpeggio Position 3

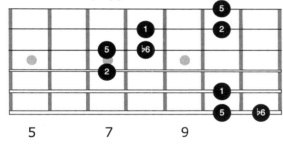

G Aeolian arpeggio Position 4

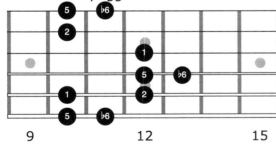

G Aeolian arpeggio Position 5

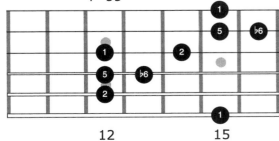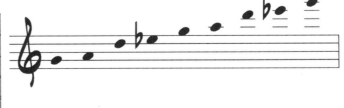

G Aeolian arpeggio Position 1

G Aeolian arpeggio Position 2

G Aeolian arpeggio Position 3

G Aeolian arpeggio Position 4

G Aeolian arpeggio Position 5

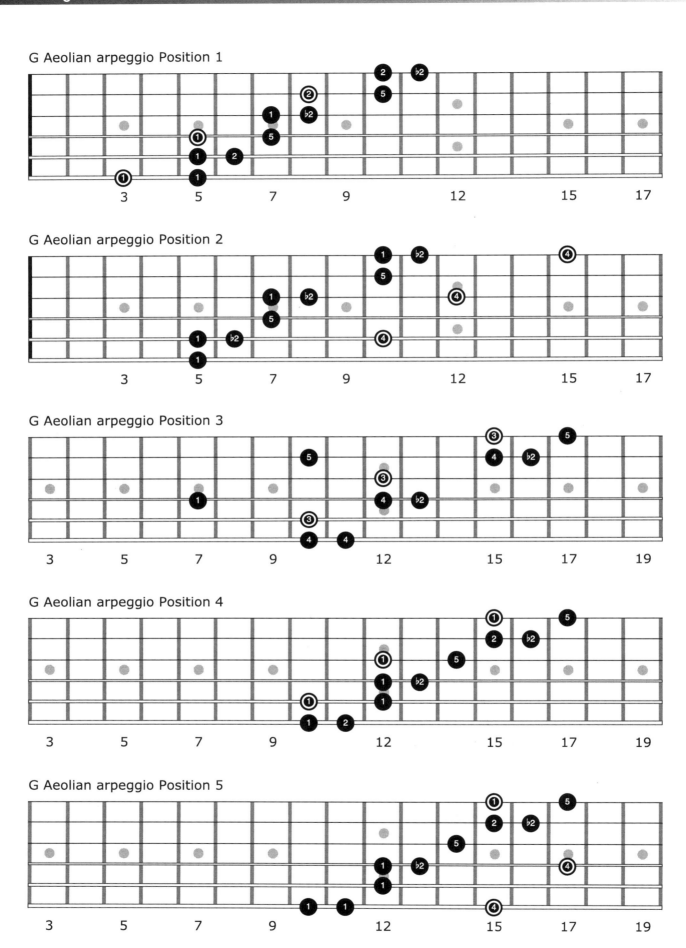

- This one should be played chord-melody style
- It only uses one parent scale - Hungarian Minor (also known as Double Harmonic Minor or Harmonic Minor #4). Asus(b6) is used often.
- As an experiment, record the chord changes in a looper and improvise using A Aeolian arpeggios.
- See the reference section for Hungarian Minor scale shapes, & modal relatives with voicing options.

Aeolian Etude #1

Noel Johnston

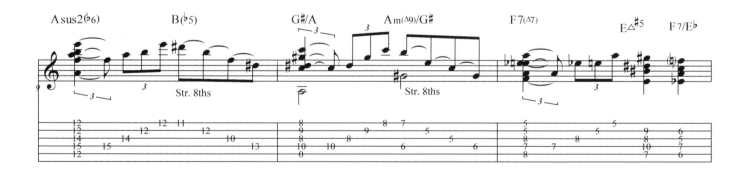

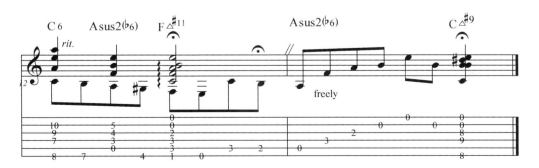

- This one uses modal Aeolian arpeggios (1, 2, 5, b6) with some slight variations through various aeolian sounds.
- The "aeol" chord symbols indicate sus2(b6).
- The key centers used here are the same as the tune "Cherokee."

Aeolian Etude #2

Noel Johnston

For performance examples: https://www.youtube.com/user/nohjoh08

The "Magic 6th" Voicing

What is the "Magic 6th" Voicing?

•It's a Major 7th voicing with an added 6th, but no 5th.
•The name is made up, but it is an extremely flavorful and adaptable voicing.
•Even though it has a 3rd and a 7th, it is not exactly a tertian voicing.
•This Magic 6th voicing (1, 3, 6, 7), other than the root, uses the notes left out of the Phrygian voicing (1, ♭2, 4, 5)
•Descending from the 7, it is the "Cry me a River" lick.

•It has both functional and modal qualities (can be used in a progression or as a static sound) depending on context.

The following pages contain chord and arpeggio shapes for the "Magic 6th" voicing (1, 3, 6, 7) and the multiple possibilities that can result from assigning those essential tones.

F6△7 (no 5th) "Magic 6th"

The "Magic 6th"

FMaj6△7 (no 5th) <or> Dm(add2)/F

"Essence" of this voicing: **1,** ♮**3,** ♮**6,** ♮**7.**

(These notes would make up the SHELL VOICING and the basic arpeggio)

The non-essential tones are: ♮**2 or** ♯**2**

(these notes are the color tones or upper extensions)   ♮**4 or** ♯**4**

♮**5 or** ♯**5**

With those variables, there are 8 possible combinations:

♮2 ♮4 ♮5 *

♯2 ♮4 ♮5

♮2 ♯4 ♮5 *

♮2 ♮4 ♯5 *

♯2 ♮4 ♯5 *

♯2 ♯4 ♮5 *

♮2 ♯4 ♯5 *

♯2 ♯4 ♯5 *

(* indicates sounds that are less obscure and more 'useful' than the others)

Here are 7 *useful* sounds that work with this voicing:

1, ♮**2,** ♮3, ♮**4,** ♮**5,** ♮**6,** ♮7 (Major scale - Ionian)

1, ♮**2,** ♮3, ♯**4,** ♮**5,** ♮**6,** ♮7 (Lydian - 4th mode of Major scale)

1, ♮**2,** ♮3, ♮**4,** ♯**5,** ♮**6,** ♮7 (Ionian #5 - 3rd mode of Harmonic minor)

1, ♯**2,** ♮3, ♮**4,** ♯**5,** ♮**6,** ♮7 (3rd mode Hungarian min/Double harmonic min, or 6th mode dbl harm maj)

1, ♯**2,** ♮3, ♯**4,** ♮**5,** ♮**6,** ♮7 (Lydian #9 - 6th mode of Harmonic minor)

1, ♮**2,** ♮3, ♯**4,** ♯**5,** ♮**6,** ♮7 (Lydian-Augmented - 3rd mode of Melodic minor)

1, ♯**2,** ♮3, ♯**4,** ♯**5,** ♮**6,** ♮7 (Lydian #9 #5 - 6th mode of Harmonic major)

I. F Major (Ionian)

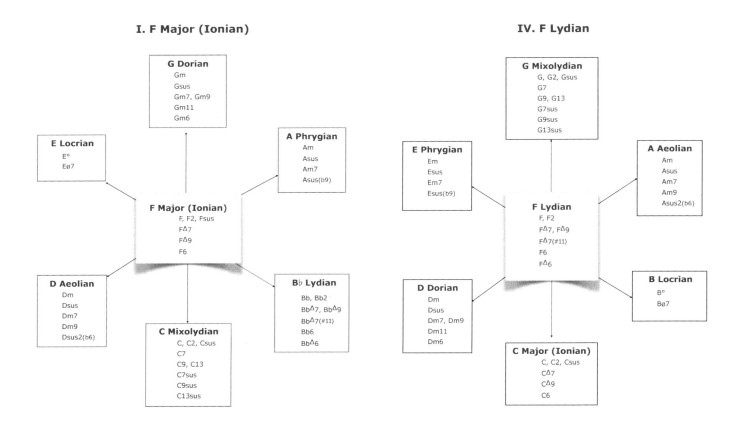

G Dorian
Gm
Gsus
Gm7, Gm9
Gm11
Gm6

E Locrian
E°
Eø7

A Phrygian
Am
Asus
Am7
Asus(b9)

F Major (Ionian)
F, F2, Fsus
FΔ7
FΔ9
F6

D Aeolian
Dm
Dsus
Dm7
Dm9
Dsus2(b6)

Bb Lydian
Bb, Bb2
BbΔ7, BbΔ9
BbΔ7(#11)
Bb6
BbΔ6

C Mixolydian
C, C2, Csus
C7
C9, C13
C7sus
C9sus
C13sus

IV. F Lydian

G Mixolydian
G, G2, Gsus
G7
G9, G13
G7sus
G9sus
G13sus

E Phrygian
Em
Esus
Em7
Esus(b9)

A Aeolian
Am
Asus
Am7
Am9
Asus2(b6)

F Lydian
F, F2
FΔ7, FΔ9
FΔ7(#11)
F6
FΔ6

D Dorian
Dm
Dsus
Dm7, Dm9
Dm11
Dm6

B Locrian
B°
Bø7

C Major (Ionian)
C, C2, Csus
CΔ7
CΔ9
C6

III. F Ionian #5

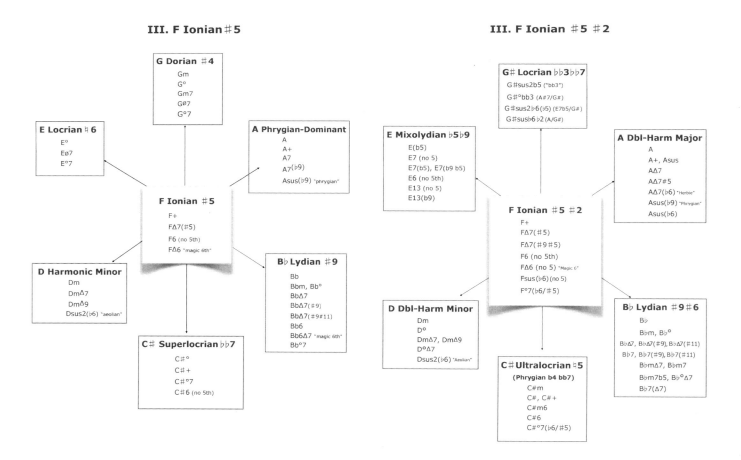

G Dorian #4
Gm
G°
Gm7
Gø7
G°7

E Locrian ♮6
E°
Eø7
E°7

A Phrygian-Dominant
A
A+
A7
A7(b9)
Asus(b9) "phrygian"

F Ionian #5
F+
FΔ7(#5)
F6 (no 5th)
FΔ6 "magic 6th"

D Harmonic Minor
Dm
DmΔ7
DmΔ9
Dsus2(b6) "aeolian"

Bb Lydian #9
Bb
Bbm, Bb°
BbΔ7
BbΔ7(#9)
BbΔ7(#9#11)
Bb6
Bb6Δ7 "magic 6th"
Bb°7

C# Superlocrian bb7
C#°
C#+
C#°7
C#6 (no 5th)

III. F Ionian #5 #2

G# Locrian bb3bb7
G#sus2b5 ("bb3")
G#°bb3 (A#7/G#)
G#sus2b6(b5) (E7b5/G#)
G#susb6b2 (A/G#)

E Mixolydian b5b9
E(b5)
E7 (no 5)
E7(b5), E7(b9 b5)
E6 (no 5th)
E13 (no 5)
E13(b9)

A Dbl-Harm Major
A
A+, Asus
AΔ7
AΔ7#5
AΔ7(b6) "Herbie"
Asus(b9) "Phrygian"
Asus(b6)

F Ionian #5 #2
F+
FΔ7(#5)
FΔ7(#9#5)
F6 (no 5th)
FΔ6 (no 5) "Magic 6"
Fsus(b6)(no 5)
F°7(b6/#5)

D Dbl-Harm Minor
Dm
D°
DmΔ7, DmΔ9
D°Δ7
Dsus2(b6) "Aeolian"

Bb Lydian #9#6
Bb
Bbm, Bb°
BbΔ7, BbΔ7(#9), BbΔ7(#11)
Bb7, Bb7(#9), Bb7(#11)
BbmΔ7, Bbm7
Bbm7b5, Bb°Δ7
Bb7(Δ7)

C# Ultralocrian ♮5
(Phrygian b4 bb7)
C#m
C#, C#+
C#m6
C#6
C#°7(b6/#5)

VI. F Lydian ♯9

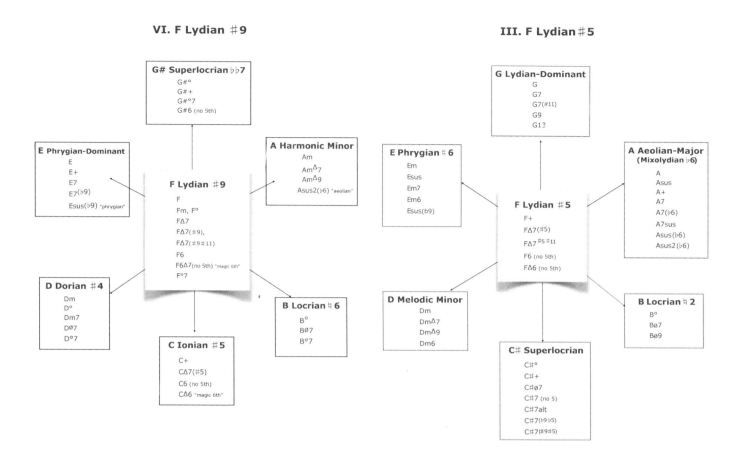

G♯ Superlocrian ♭♭7
G♯°
G♯+
G♯°7
G♯6 (no 5th)

E Phrygian-Dominant
E
E+
E7
E7(♭9)
Esus(♭9) "phrygian"

A Harmonic Minor
Am
AmΔ7
AmΔ9
Asus2(♭6) "aeolian"

F Lydian ♯9
F
Fm, F°
FΔ7
FΔ7(♯9),
FΔ7(♯9♯11)
F6
F6Δ7(no 5th) "magic 6th"
F°7

D Dorian ♯4
Dm
D°
Dm7
DØ7
D°7

B Locrian ♮6
B°
BØ7
B°7

C Ionian ♯5
C+
CΔ7(♯5)
C6 (no 5th)
CΔ6 "magic 6th"

III. F Lydian ♯5

G Lydian-Dominant
G
G7
G7(♯11)
G9
G13

E Phrygian ♮6
Em
Esus
Em7
Em6
Esus(♭9)

A Aeolian-Major
(Mixolydian ♭6)
A
Asus
A+
A7
A7(♭6)
A7sus
Asus(♭6)
Asus2(♭6)

F Lydian ♯5
F+
FΔ7(♯5)
FΔ7 ♯5 ♯11
F6 (no 5th)
FΔ6 (no 5th)

D Melodic Minor
Dm
DmΔ7
DmΔ9
Dm6

B Locrian ♮2
B°
BØ7
BØ9

C♯ Superlocrian
C♯°
C♯+
C♯Ø7
C♯7 (no 5)
C♯7alt
C♯7(♭9♭5)
C♯7(♯9♯5)

VI. F Lydian-Aug ♯2

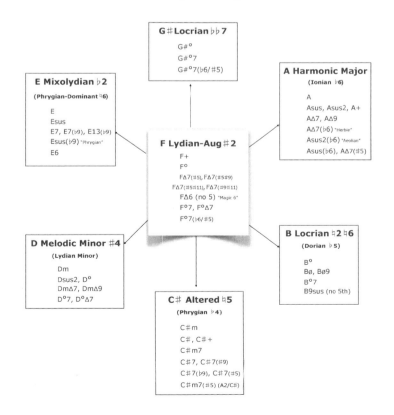

G♯ Locrian ♭♭7
G♯°
G♯°7
G♯°7(♭6/♯5)

E Mixolydian ♭2
(Phrygian-Dominant ♮6)
E
Esus
E7, E7(♭9), E13(♭9)
Esus(♭9) "Phrygian"
E6

A Harmonic Major
(Ionian ♭6)
A
Asus, Asus2, A+
AΔ7, AΔ9
AΔ7(♭6) "Herbie"
Asus2(♭6) "Aeolian"
Asus(♭6), AΔ7(♯5)

F Lydian-Aug ♯2
F+
F°
FΔ7(♯5), FΔ7(♯5♯9)
FΔ7(♯5♯11), FΔ7(♯9♯11)
FΔ6 (no 5) "Magic 6"
F°7, F°Δ7
F°7(♭6/♯5)

D Melodic Minor ♯4
(Lydian Minor)
Dm
Dsus2, D°
DmΔ7, DmΔ9
D°7, D°Δ7

B Locrian ♮2♮6
(Dorian ♭5)
B°
BØ, BØ9
B°7
B9sus (no 5th)

C♯ Altered ♮5
(Phrygian ♭4)
C♯m
C♯, C♯+
C♯m7
C♯7, C♯7(♯9)
C♯7(♭9), C♯7(♯5)
C♯m7(♯5) (A2/C♯)

Larger size modal relative diagrams are in the reference section of this book starting pg. 72.

For interactive modal relative diagrams, download the "Voicing Modes" iOS app, or "Voicing Modes" web app at www.noeljohnston.com

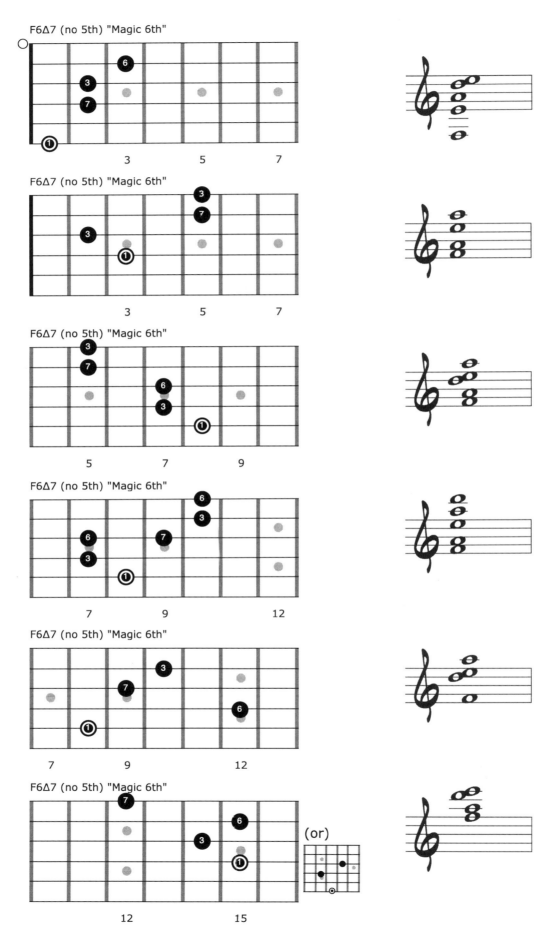

30

F Magic 6th arpeggio Position 1

F Magic 6th arpeggio Position 2

F Magic 6th arpeggio Position 3

F Magic 6th arpeggio Position 4

F Magic 6th arpeggio Position 4b

F Magic 6th arpeggio Position 5

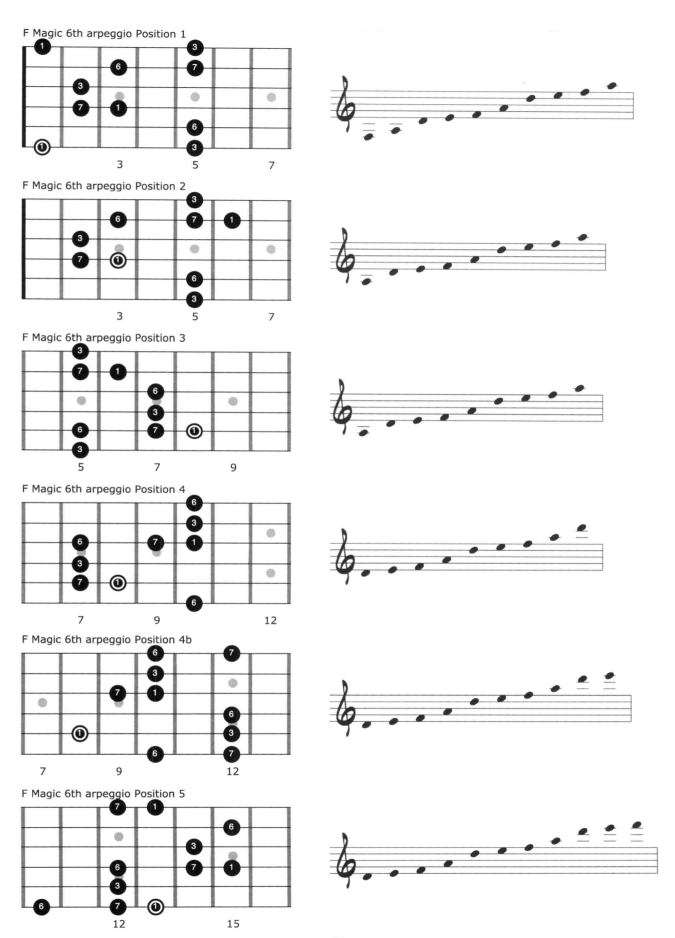

F "Magic 6th" arpeggio Position 2

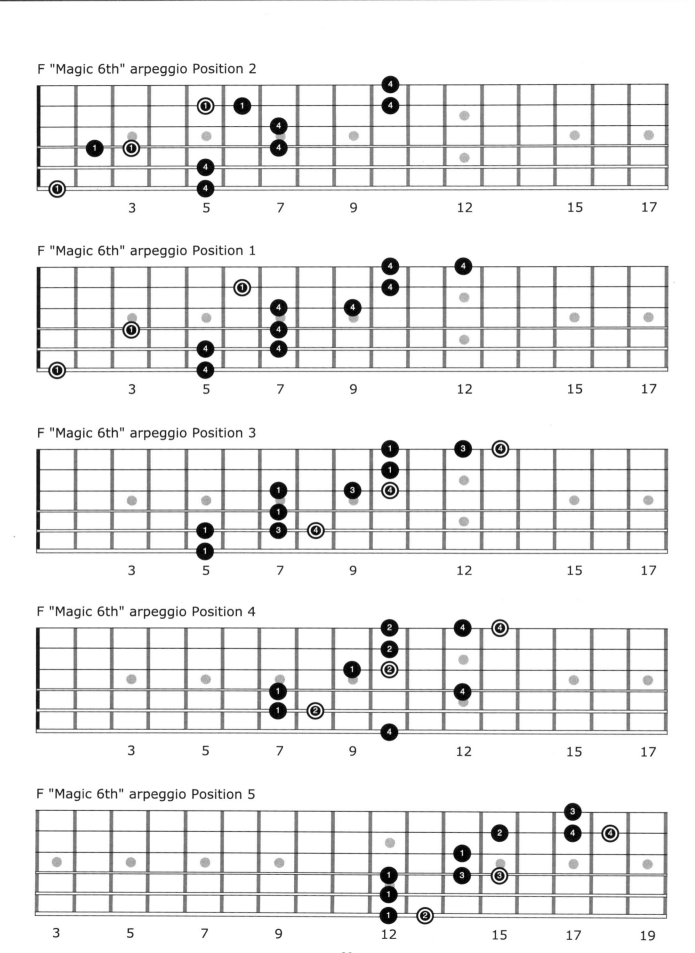

F "Magic 6th" arpeggio Position 1

F "Magic 6th" arpeggio Position 3

F "Magic 6th" arpeggio Position 4

F "Magic 6th" arpeggio Position 5

- This one sticks to only 1-3-6-7 voicings. Both chords and lines.
- The chord shapes and lines are supposed to mirror each other on the same place on the neck (and are suggested fingerings/positions - feel free to come up with your own *sustained* arrangement). I call this the "Jim Hall Method" - where lines and chords are conceived in the same part of the brain. As with the other etudes, try to think of these lines as voicings instead of just single-line 'shred' arpeggios. Guitar as a hybrid line/chord instrument is unique in this way.
- The tune, harmonically, only uses three key centers: B, G, & Eb. (Giant Steps) The Magic 6th voicing works on the I & IV chords of each key. See page 47-51 for more Giant Steps modal reharmonization for comping over this etude.

Magic 6th Etude #1

Noel Johnston

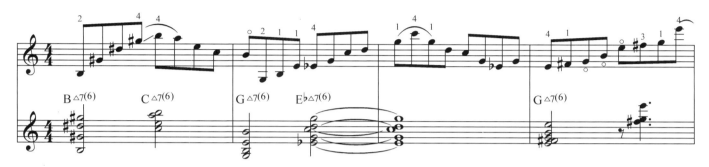

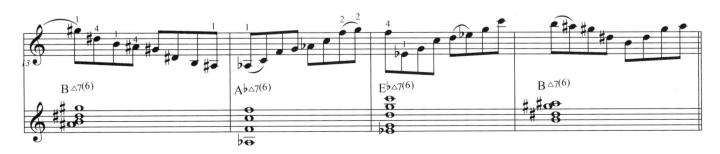

- This one uses mostly "Magic 6th" (1-3-6-7) voicings appropriate for the key centers of the tune, "Alone together."
- Key centers used in order of appearance: F major, D harmonic minor, Bb major, G harmonic minor, A major, D major, F harmonic major, C major, F melodic minor.

Magic 6th Etude #2

Noel Johnston

Modal Becoming Functional

Enharmonic equivalence

Some sounds, when "modally voiced" (with upper extensions in a lower register) can actually become functional. In other words, some modes contain 2nds, 4ths, or 6ths which are enharmonically equivalent to intervals that make up common sounding triads and seventh chords.

$\sharp2 = \flat3$

$\flat4 = \natural3$

$\sharp4 = \flat5$

$\flat6 = \flat5$

$\natural6 = \flat\flat7$, and so on.

▫Example 1: The F Lydian #9 mode (6th mode of A harmonic Minor):

1, ♯2, 3, ♯4, 5, 6, 7

1-3-5 triad is an *F Major triad*
1-♯2-5 is "Fsus ♯2" which is enharmonically equivalent to an *F Minor triad.*
1-♯2-♯4 is "Fsus ♯4 add ♯2 (no 5th)" which is enharmonically equivalent to an *F° triad*
Similarly,
1-3-5-7 is *FΔ7*
1-♯2-5-7 "FΔ7sus#2" (who wants to read that?!) is enharmonically equivalent to an *FmΔ7*
1-♯2-♯4-7 "Fsus#4Δ7 add#2 no 5th" (boo!) is enharmonically equivalent to an *F°Δ7*
1-♯2-♯4-6 "F6sus#4#2 no 5th" (yikes!) is enharmonically equivalent to an *F°7*

▫Example 2: Super Locrian/Altered (7th mode of Melodic Minor):

1, ♭2, ♭3, ♭4, ♭5, ♭6, ♭7

When voiced in 3rds, it is a Half-Diminished chord: 1, ♭3, ♭5, ♭7
BUT... if you voice the ♭4 as foundational, it's perceived as a ♮3rd - and against the ♭7 it makes the dissonant tritone - the most common way to voice this sound is actually a DOMINANT 7th sound:

1, ♮3, ♭7 (♭9, ♯9, ♭5, ♯5) ("Fully Altered")

▫Example 3: Superlocrian ♭♭7 (7th mode of Harmonic Minor):

1, ♭2, ♭3, ♭4, ♭5, ♭6, ♭♭7

When voiced in 3rds, it is a Fully-Diminished chord: 1, ♭3, ♭5, ♭♭7
BUT... if you voice the ♭4 as foundational, it's perceived it as a ♮3rd - making it a major voicing - and the ♭♭7 then sounds like a ♮6 making the voicing a MAJOR 6th sound:

1, ♮3, ♮6, (♯5, ♯11)

With that in mind, check out these 8 different diminished flavors of Harmonic Minor and Harmonic Major:

The 4 Diminished flavors in Harmonic Minor

G Locrian ♮6

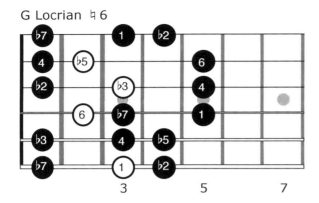

2nd mode: Voiced in 3rds it is a ø7, but it can also be voiced as a °7

6 = enharmonic bb7

Tertian: ø7
Modal: °7
Cadence/Triad Pair: Fm <--> G°
Blues: minor blues (no ♮5)

G Dorian #4

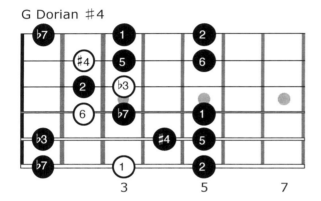

4th mode: Voiced in 3rds it is a m7, but it can also be voiced as a ø7, or °7

#4 = enharmonic b5
6 = enharmonic bb7

Tertian: m7
Modal: °7, ø7
T/P: Dm <--> G°
Blues: minor blues (no ♮4)

G Lydian #9

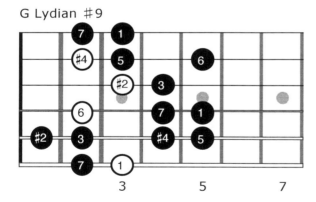

6th mode: Voiced in 3rds it is a Δ7 & Δ7(#9), but it can also be voiced as a m6, or °7

#2 = enharmonic b3
#4 = enharmonic b5
6 = enharmonic bb7

Tertian: Δ7, Δ7#9, Δ7#9#11
Modal: °7, 6th, m6, min triad.
T/P: Bm <--> G°
Blues: minor blues (no ♭7, no ♮4)

G Superlocrian bb7

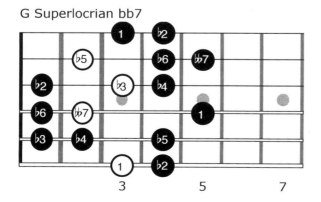

7th mode: Voiced in 3rds it is a °7, but it can also be voiced as a Maj6 (no 5), and an Augmented triad.

b4 = enharmonic 3
bb7 = enharmonic 6
b6 = enharmonic #5

Tertian: °7
Modal: Maj6(no5), Aug triad
T/P: Abm <--> G°

The 4 Diminished flavors in Harmonic Major

G Locrian ♮2♮6

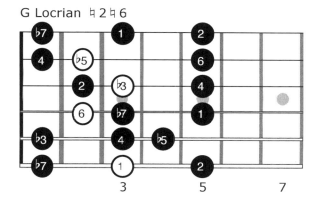

2nd mode: Voiced in 3rds it is a ø7, but it can also be voiced as a °7

6 = enharmonic bb7

Tertian: ø7
Modal: °7
Cadence/Triad Pair: F <--> G°
Blues: minor blues (no ♮5)

G Lydian-Minor

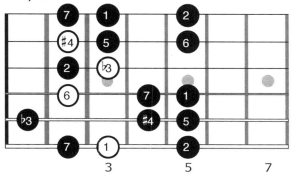

4th mode: Voiced in 3rds it is a mΔ7, but it can also be voiced as a m6, or °7

#4 = enharmonic b5
6 = enharmonic bb7

Tertian: mΔ7
Modal: °7, ø7
T/P: D <--> G°
Blues: minor blues (no ♭7, no ♮4)

G Lydian #5#9

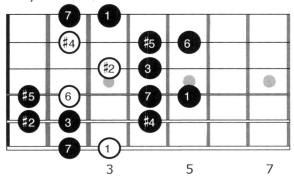

6th mode: Voiced in 3rds it is a Δ7#5 & Δ7#5(#9), but it can also be voiced as a 6Δ7(no5), or °7

#2 = enharmonic b3
#4 = enharmonic b5
6 = enharmonic bb7

Tertian: Δ7, Δ7#9, Δ7#9#11
Modal: °7, 6th, m6, min triad.
T/P: B <--> G°

G Locrian bb7

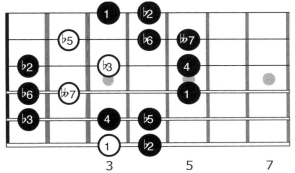

7th mode: Voiced in 3rds it is a °7,

bb7 = enharmonic 6
b6 = enharmonic #5

Tertian: °7
Modal: Maj6(no5), Aug triad
T/P: Ab <--> G°

Just to let those variations sink in a bit more, check out this very guitaristic fingering of these various diminished sounds. Compare them to the symmetrical diminished.
Some of these sounds are very useable in the context of minor blues licks.

Diminished idea #1
°7 arpeggio on B & D strings, with flavor notes on G-string

Whole-1/2 Diminished

G° whole-1/2 Diminished Scale - G°, Bb°, Db°, Fb°

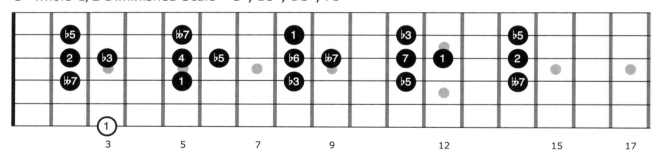

1/2-Whole Diminished

G° 1/2-Whole Diminished Scale - G7, Bb7, C#7, E7

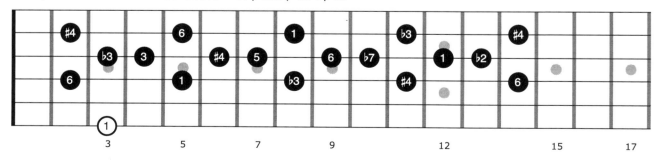

Harmonic Minor

G Ultralocrian (Ab Harmonic Minor) - G°, Bb°, Db°, Fb°

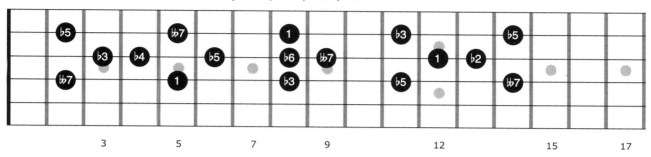

G Locrian ♮6 (F Harmonic Minor) - G°, Bb°, Db°, E°

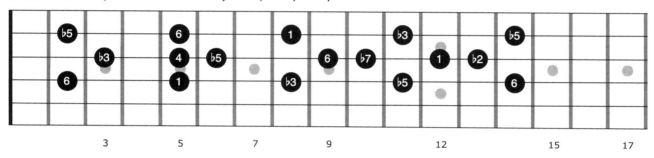

G Dorian #4 (D Harmonic Minor) - G°, Bb°, C#°, E°

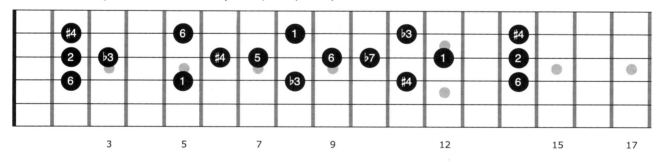

G Lydian #9 (B Harmonic Minor) - G°, A#°, C#°, E°

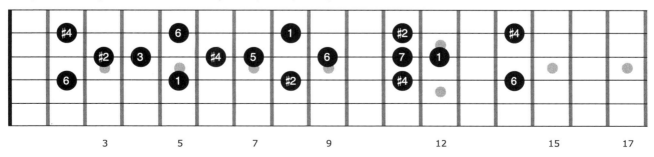

Harmonic Major

G Locrian bb7 (Ab Harmonic Major) - G°, Bb°, Db°, Fb°

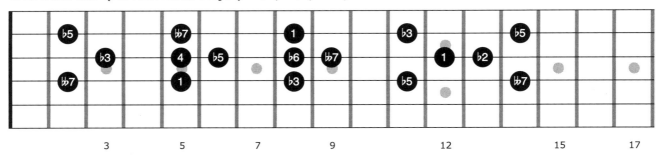

G Locrian ♮2♮6 (F Harmonic Major) - G°, Bb°, Db°, E°

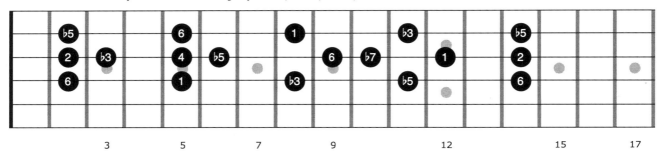

G Lydian-Minor (D Harmonic Major) - G°, Bb°, C#°, E°

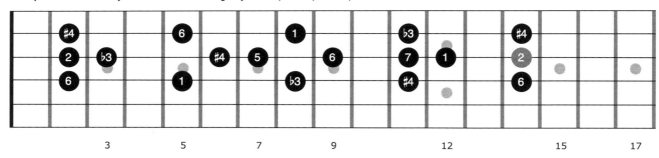

G Lydian-Augmented ♯5♯9 (B Harmonic Major) - G°, A#°, C#°, E°

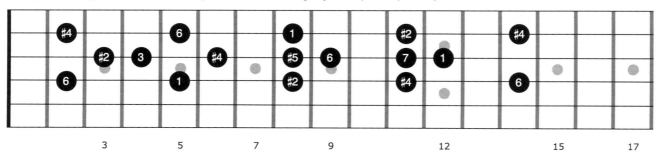

•This one descends diatonically through three key centers: A harmonic minor, Db harmonic minor, and F harmonic major) savoring each of the 4 modes in each key where a diminished chord can be played. (The vii, vi, iv, & ii)
•The differences in each diminished chord should be understood here as having a tonal context. (i.e. They are not symmetrical diminished sounds so, whole-half, or half-whole diminished scales are incorrect here)
•Rhythmically, it references a triplet-feel with a 5:3 polyrythm. 3 in the bass, 5 in the chords.

Diminished Etude #1

Noel Johnston

- Like Diminished Etude #1, this one descends diatonically through three key centers: A harmonic minor, Db harmonic minor, and F harmonic major)
- The differences in each diminished chord should be understood here as having a tonal context. (i.e. They are not symmetrical diminished sounds so, whole-half, or half-whole diminished scales are incorrect here)
- The melodic ideas over each chord here are licks/ideas/devices related by key center, so they work over the diminished chords in context.
- Tonal diminished chords, context correctly understood (as vii, vi, iv, or ii) will open up your creative options beyond diminished arpeggios & diminished scales.

Diminished Etude #2

Noel Johnston

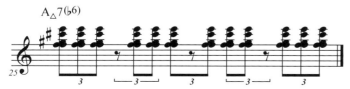

Standard Tune Examples

Following are some tune examples with reharmonized changes - the reharmonizations follow a strict adherence to the key center the composer intended. Simply put, they are just "Diatonic Substitutions." Not only can you use diatonic subs to change the accompaniment (one type of "reharmonization"), you can use them to gain new ideas for soloing over the original chord changes ("Bracketing" or "Modal Bracketing")

Reducing the changes to it's key center is called "Bracketing"* and it's often how beginning improvisers learn to solo. Changing it to other key-center related changes could be thought of as "Advanced Bracketing." Assuming you already know and hear how to make the changes, advanced bracketing can expand your vocabulary and idea pallette over a variety of tunes.**

There are two chord-melody arrangements:
1. Stella By Starlight (not reharmonized, and again with diatonic/modal substitutions)
2. All The Things You Are (diatonic/modal substitutions)

Chord changes only, with diatonic/modal substitution options:
1. Giant Steps
2. Blue Bossa

It helps to play these with a loop pedal to fully grasp the sounds.

Please note some words of caution:
1. When soloing with this concept, be sure to make the real changes if the situation calls for it.
2. When comping, be sure to play the real changes if the situation calls for it.

*For a primer on "Bracketing," See Dan Haerle's book "The Jazz Language."
**George Russell's 1953 jazz theory work, "Lydian Chromatic Concept of Tonal Organization" favors the Lydian equivalent of any given harmony. The "Advanced Bracketing" technique here is similar, but allows all seven related sounds a chance to exist.

Stella by Starlight (standard changes)

Composed by Victor Young, 1944
Arrangement: Noel Johnston

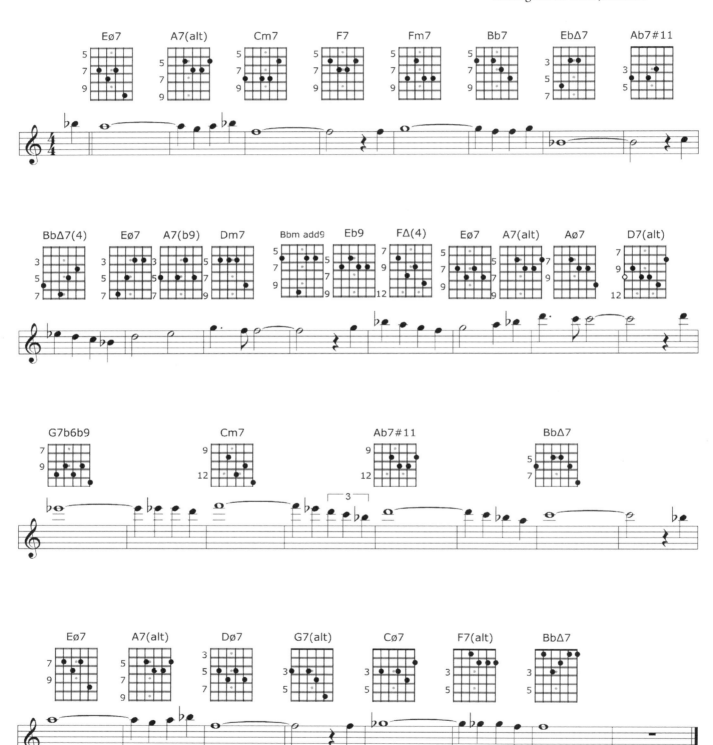

Stella by Starlight (modal sub changes)

Composed by Victor Young, 1944
Arrangement: Noel Johnston

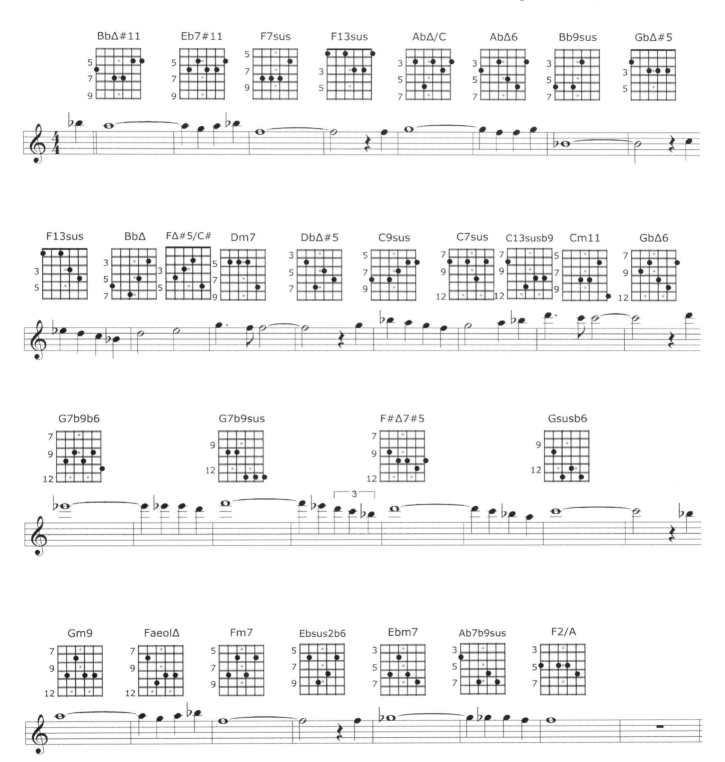

All the Things You Are (modal sub changes)

Composed by Jerome Kern, 1939
Arrangement: Noel Johnston

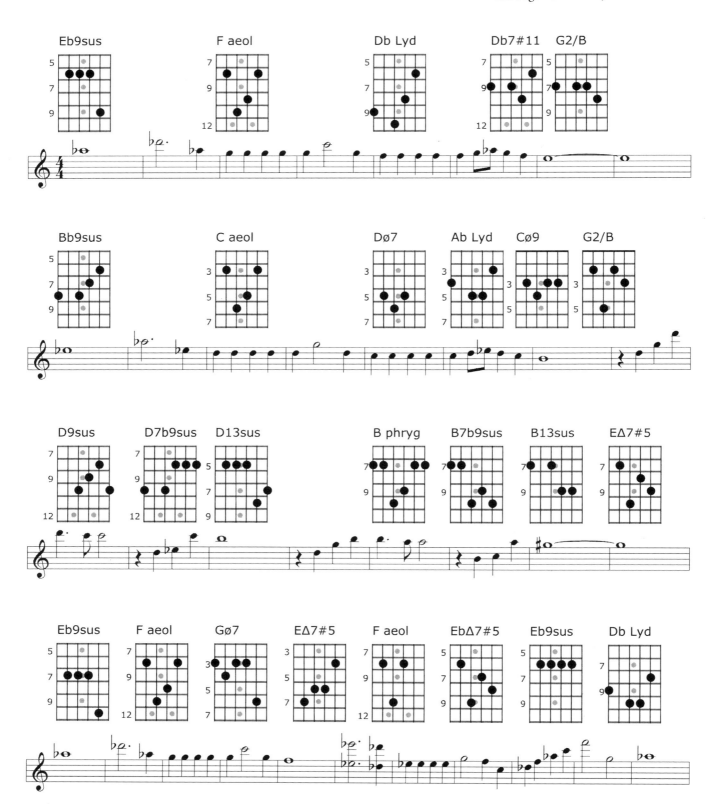

Giant Steps (original changes, and modal relatives)

Composed by John Coltrane, 1959

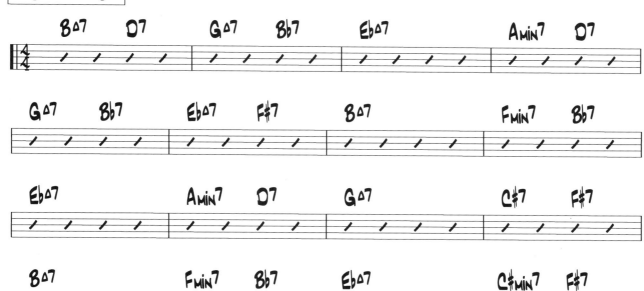

Giant Steps (diatonic modal substitutions)

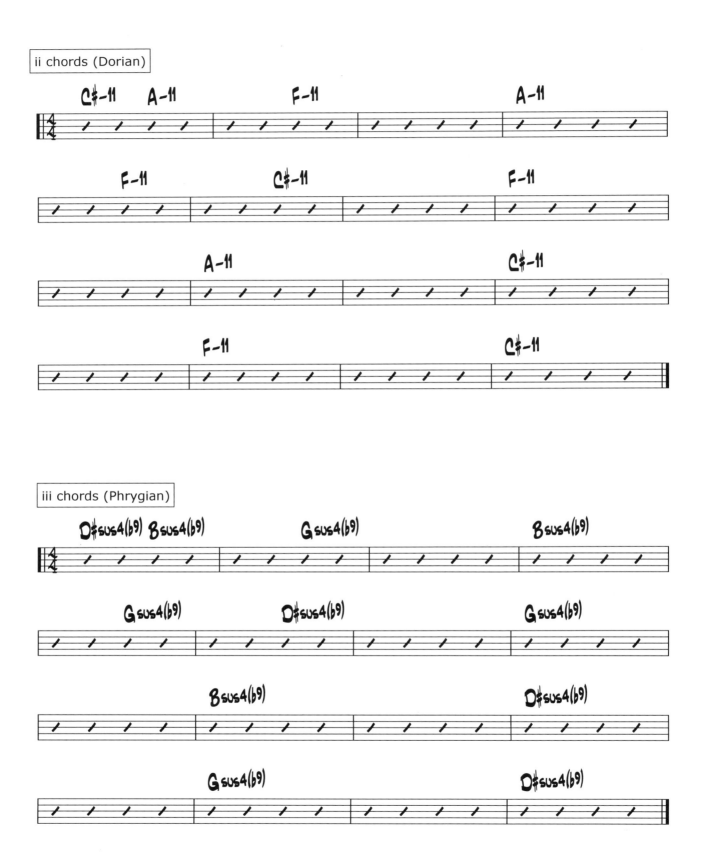

Giant Steps (diatonic modal substitutions)

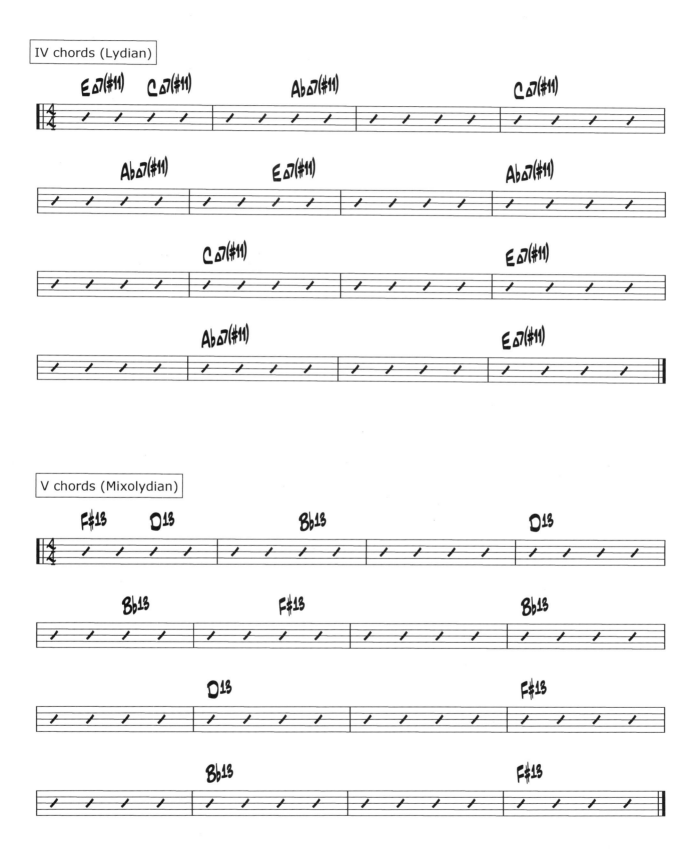

Giant Steps (diatonic modal substitutions)

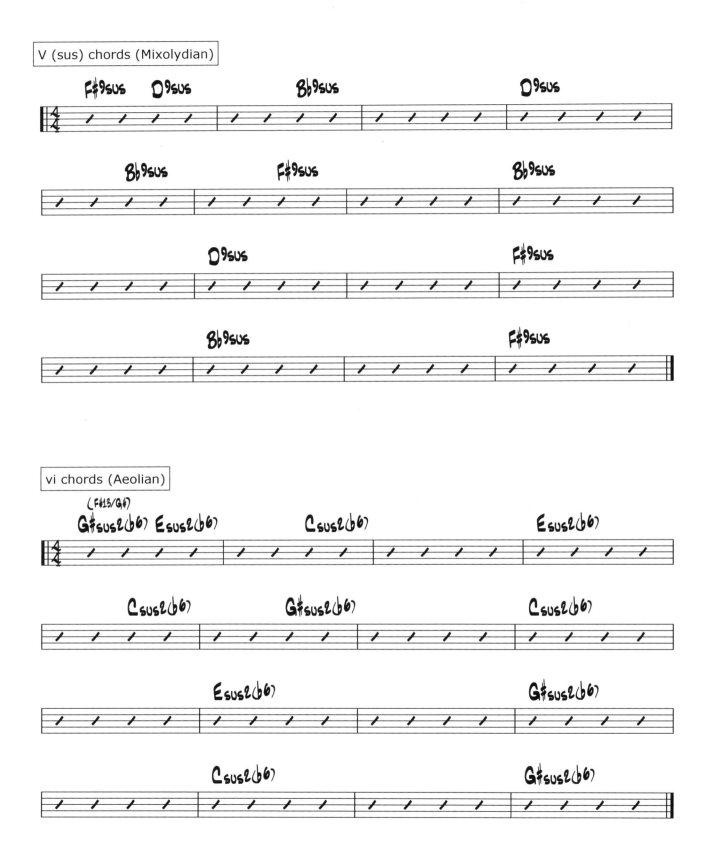

Giant Steps (diatonic modal substitutions)

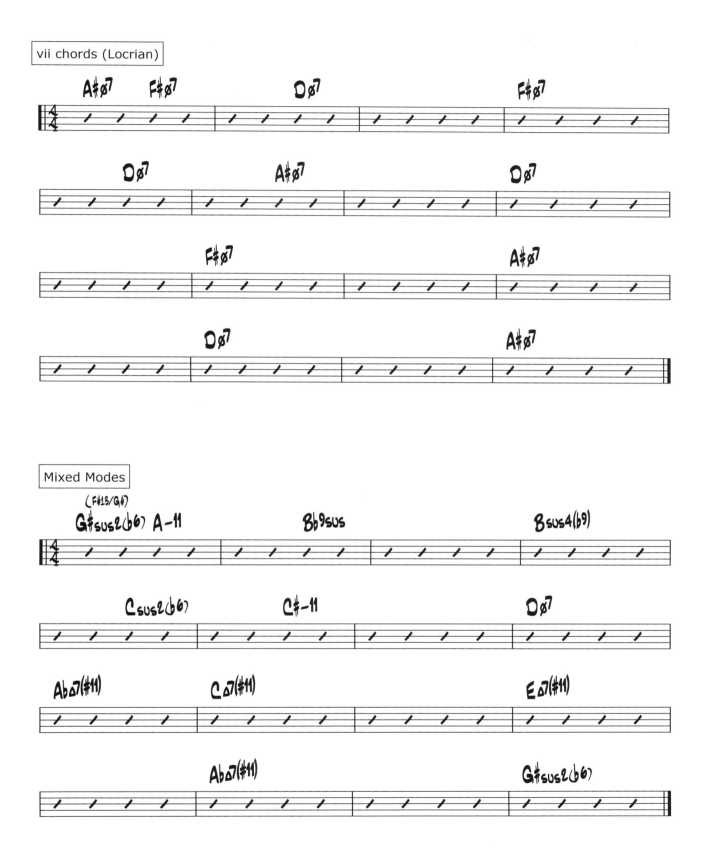

Blue Bossa (original changes, and modal relatives)

Composed by Kenny Dorham, 1963

Blue Bossa (diatonic modal substitutions)

Modal subs with G & Gb pedal

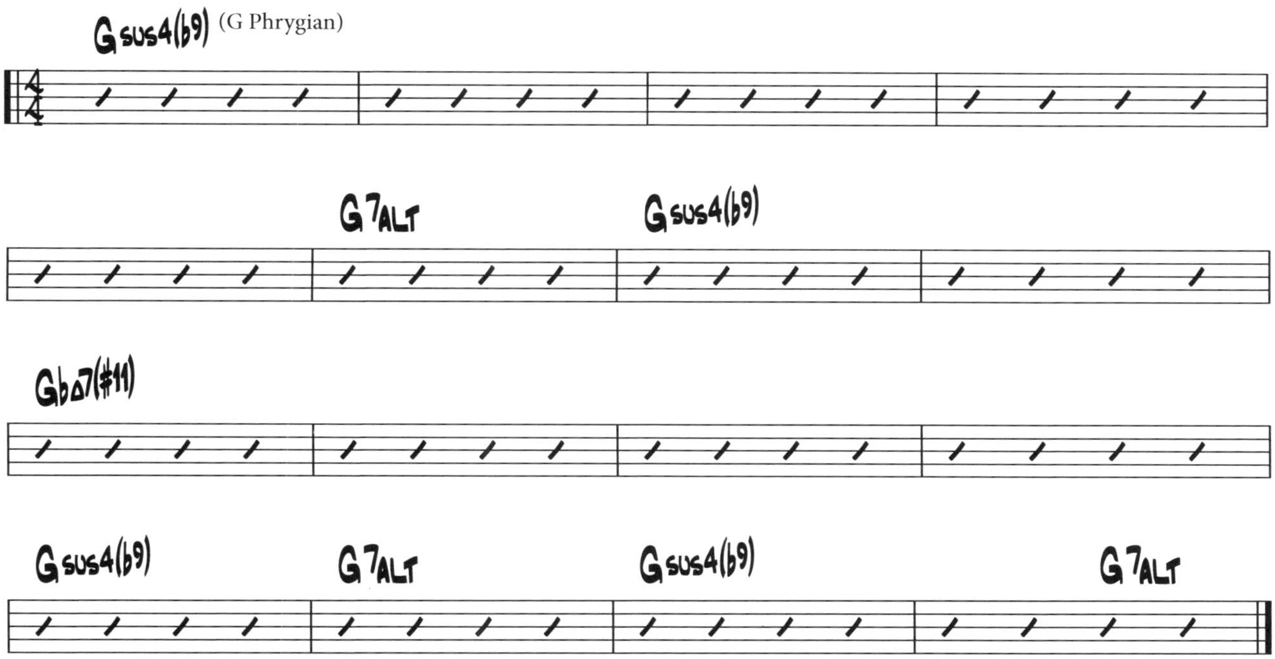

Gsus4(b9) (G Phrygian)

G7ALT **Gsus4(b9)**

Gb△7(#11)

Gsus4(b9) **G7ALT** **Gsus4(b9)** **G7ALT**

Modal subs with Ab pedal

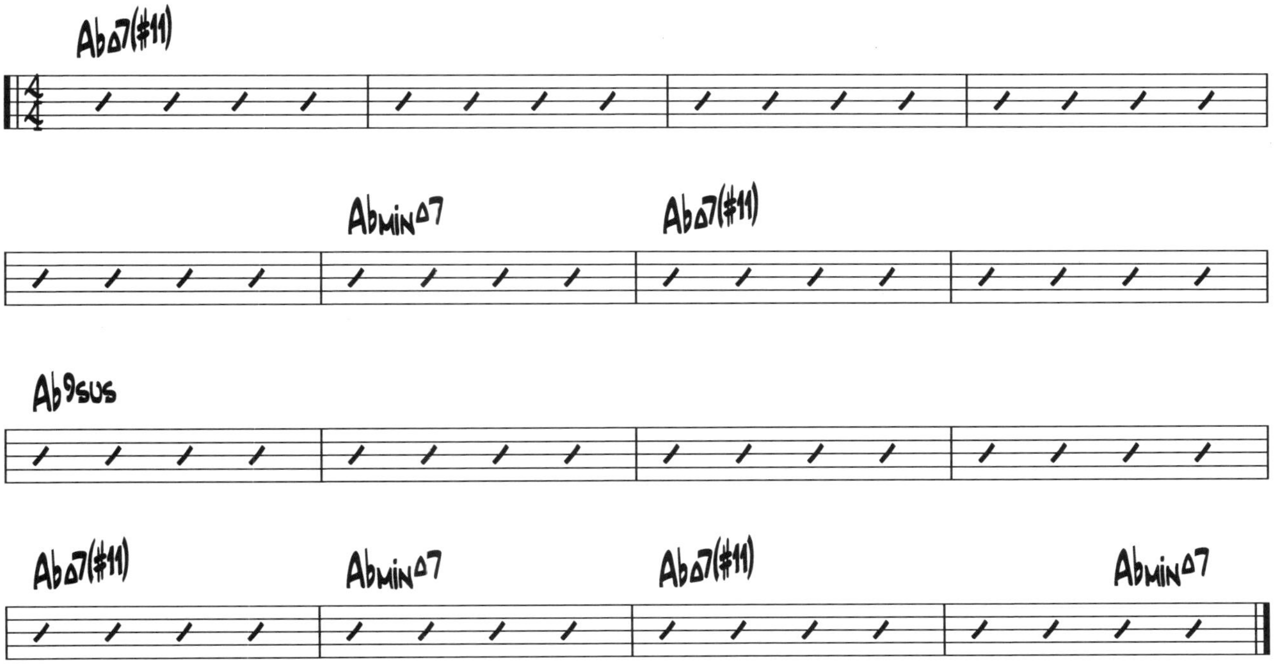

Ab△7(#11)

AbMIN△7 **Ab△7(#11)**

Ab9sus

Ab△7(#11) **AbMIN△7** **Ab△7(#11)** **AbMIN△7**

Blue Bossa (diatonic modal substitutions)

Modal subs with Bb pedal

Bb9sus

(Phrygian ♮6)
Bbsus4(b9)   **Bb9sus**

(Bb Aeolian)
Bbsus2(b6)

Bb9sus   **Bbsus4(b9)**   **Bb9sus**   **Bbsus4(b9)**

Modal subs with Eb pedal

Eb△7

(Aeolian-Major)
Abmin/Eb   **Eb△7**

Ebmin6

Eb△7   **Abmin/Eb**   **Eb△7**   **Abmin/Eb**

Blue Bossa (diatonic modal substitutions)

Reference Material

1. Sample Melodic Voicings:
Functional voicings with melodies up/down the E and B strings.

Every note in any given modal sound is harmonized with an idiomatic standard-jazz era chord voicing. Of course, there are many more options than these listed here so feel free to come up with your own harmonized scales. These are just some of my favorites.

Note: Sometimes there is a shape that aims "down the neck" and another option aiming "up the neck" - You may find the these options helpful depending on where you are on the neck.

•Practice these in multiple keys and practice them until they can be done quickly and without hesitation.
•Play these with the melody in mind. Make it beautiful.

2. Seven-position scale shapes with voicings embedded in them.

This is to help muscle-memory practice of scale shapes with easy access to harmonic context. You will notice a lot of overlapping information (the same seven shapes 7 times, for example) but the embedded chord shape will vary. Again, the embedded voicings here are just a suggestion. There are many more options possible than the ones I have listed.

To fully digest the sound of the mode you are playing, try these options:
•Play the chord shape, then play the scale up and down.
•Practice improvising around the scale shape, making sure to emphasize/accent the chord tones.
•Play the chord shape, emphasizing a melody in the shape, and continue an idea from that note.

How to read the shapes:

Melodic Voicings:

Indicates a Dominant (9th) with a 3rd in the melody on the B-string.

(no fret numbers are given as they are meant to be adaptable)

3rd

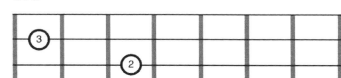

Scale Shape with voicings embedded:

Scale tones numbered in relation to F Mixolydian. Many chord shapes are possible in this shape, but the F9 is outlined.

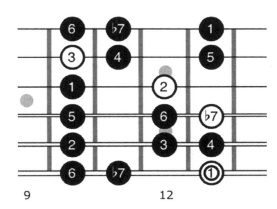

Major 7th (I/IV) - B-string Melody

EΔ7, EΔ9, EΔ13

Root

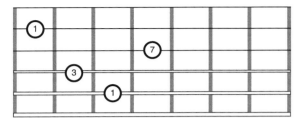

2nd/9th

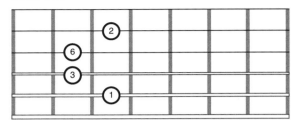

3rd

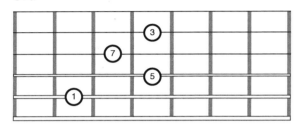

3rd

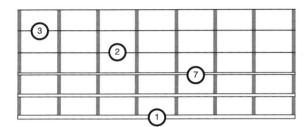

4th

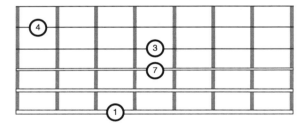

#4/#11

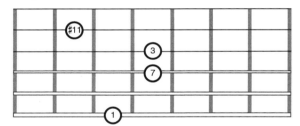

5th

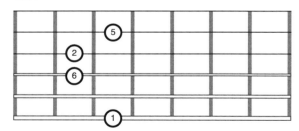

6th/13th

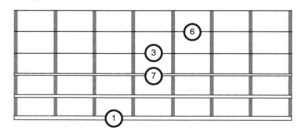

7th

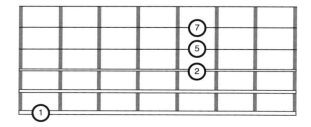

7th

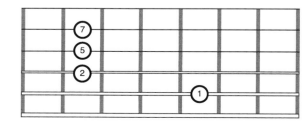

Major 7th (I/IV) - E-string Melody

EΔ7, EΔ9, EΔ13

Root

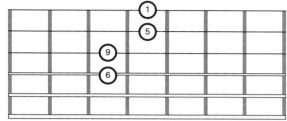

9th

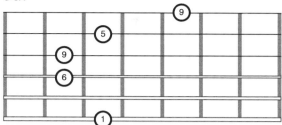

3rd

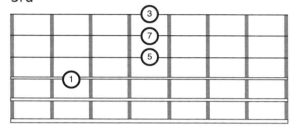

3rd

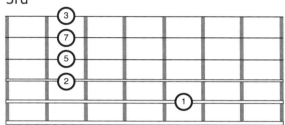

#11

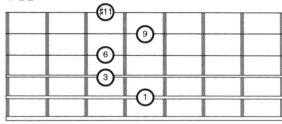

5th

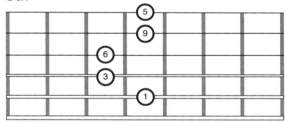

6th/13th

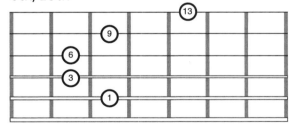

13th

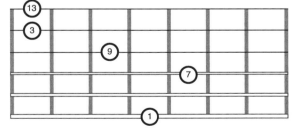

7th

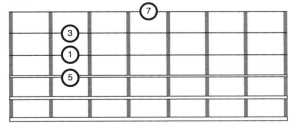

7th

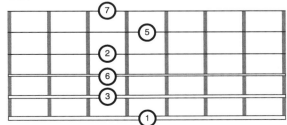

Dominant 7th (V) - B-string Melody   E7, E9, E13

Root

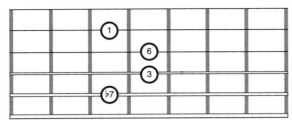

9th

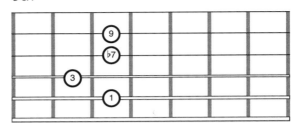

3rd

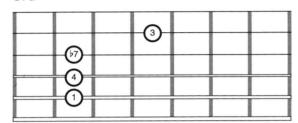

3rd

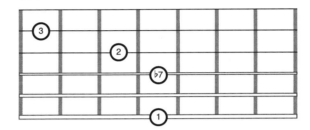

4th

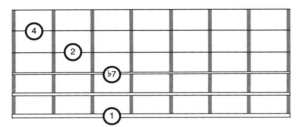

5th

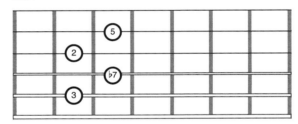

13th

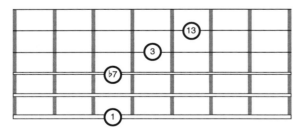

b7th

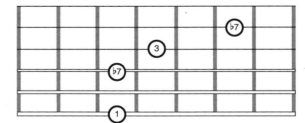

Dominant 7th (V) - E-string Melody   E7, E9, E13

Root
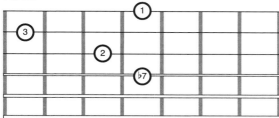

Root
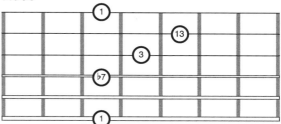

9th
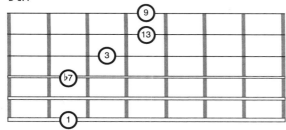

3rd
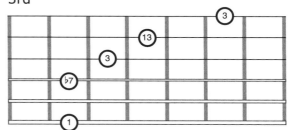

3rd
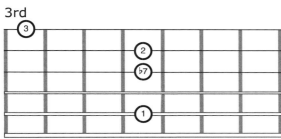

4th
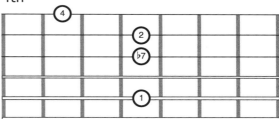

5th
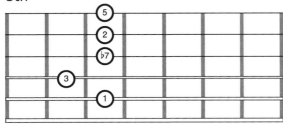

13th
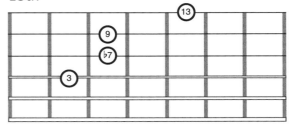

b7th
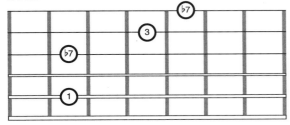

b7th
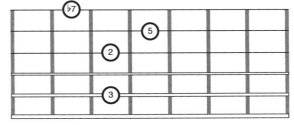

Minor 7th (ii) - B-string Melody

Em7, Em9, Em11

Root

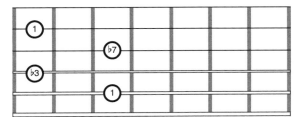

9th

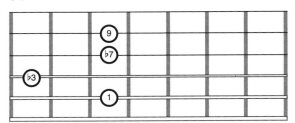

b3rd

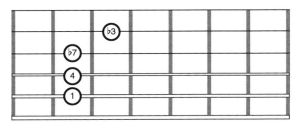

11th

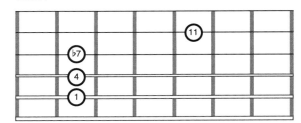

11th

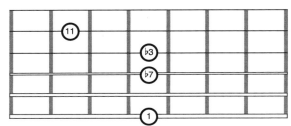

5th

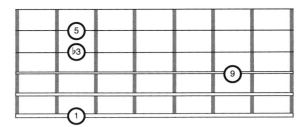

6th/13th

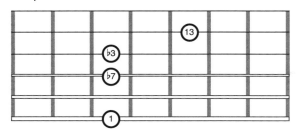

b7th

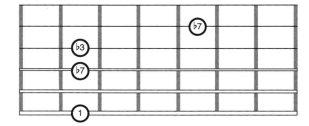

Minor 7th (ii) - E-string Melody

Em7, Em9, Em11

Root

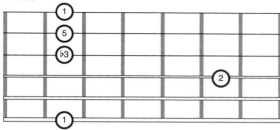

9th

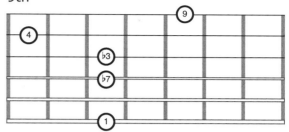

9th

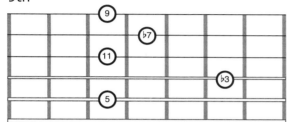

3rd

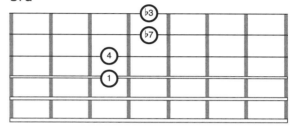

11th

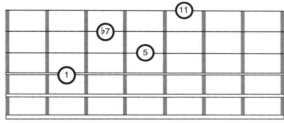

11th

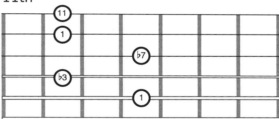

5th

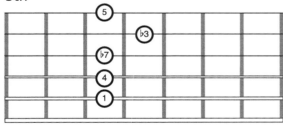

13th

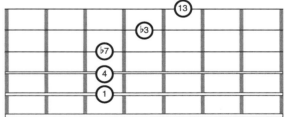

b7th

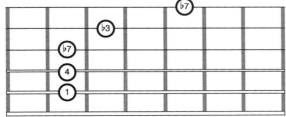

b7th

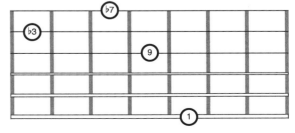

Minor 7b5/E∅7 (vii) - B-string Melody   Em7b5 - E∅7

Root

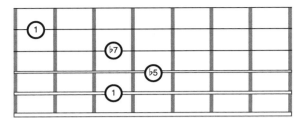

b2

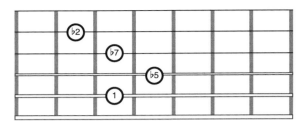

b3

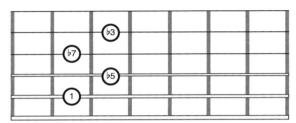

4/11

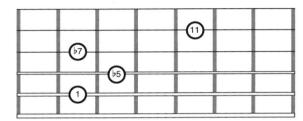

4/11

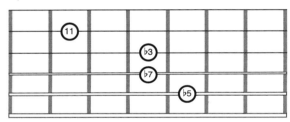

b5

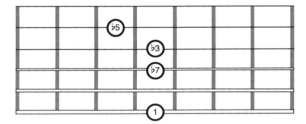

b6/b13

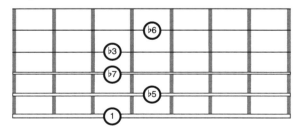

b7

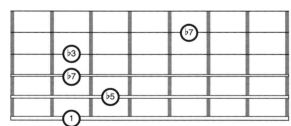

b7

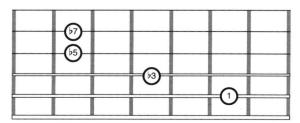

Minor 7b5/Eø7 (vii) - E-string Melody   Em7b5 - Eø7

Root

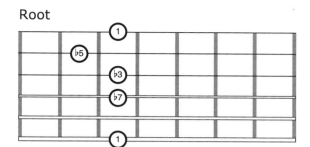

Root

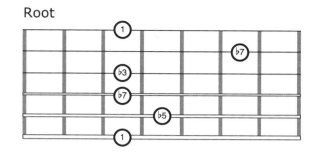

b2

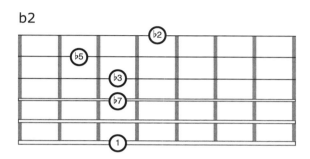

b3

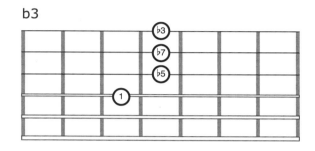

4/11

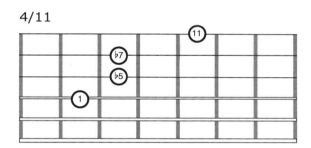

4/11

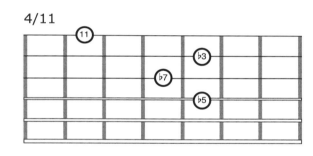

b5

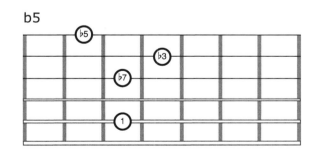

b6/b13

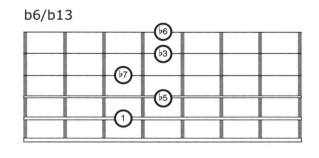

b7th

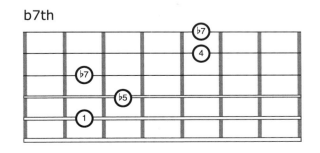

b7th

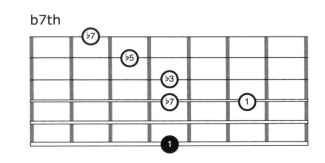

Dominant 7th (Superlocrian / Altered) - B-string Melody   E7alt

Root

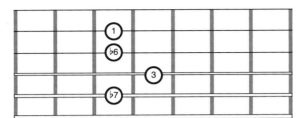

b2

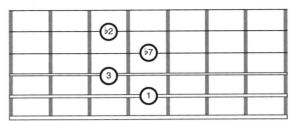

#9

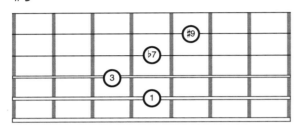

#9

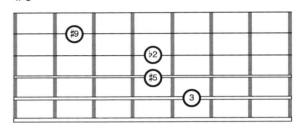

3

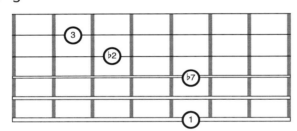

b5

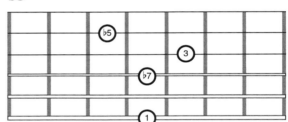

#5

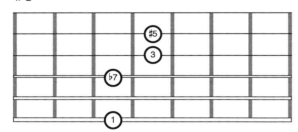

b7

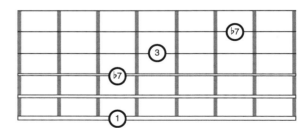

Dominant 7th (Superlocrian / Altered) - E-string Melody   E7alt

Root

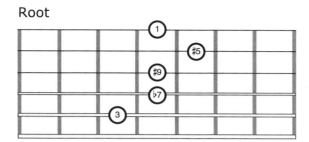

Root / b9

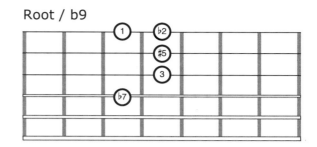

#9

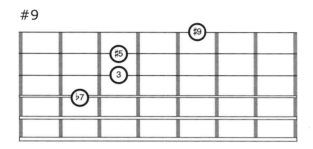

#9

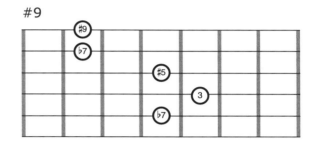

3rd

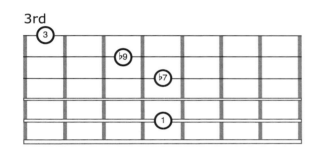

b5

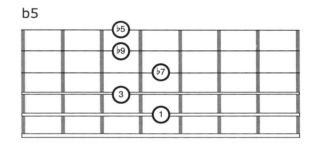

#5

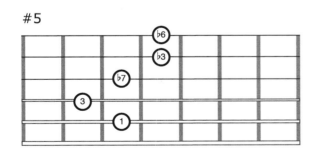

#5

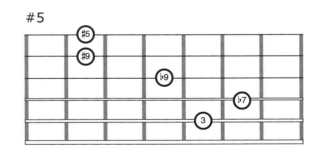

b7th

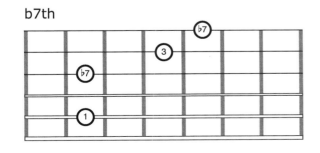

b7th

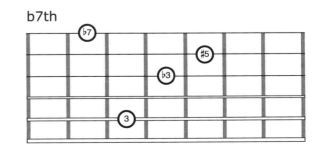

Dominant 7th - Lydian Dominant - B-string Melody

E7#11

Root

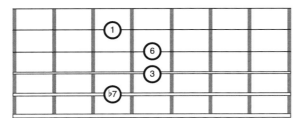

9th

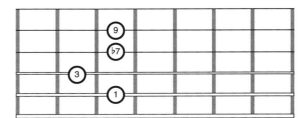

3rd

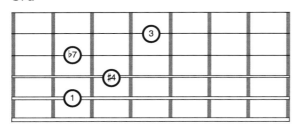

3rd

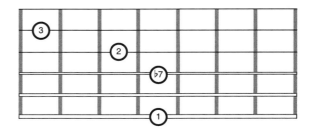

4th

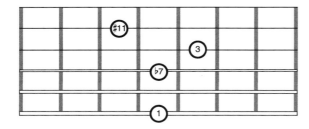

5th

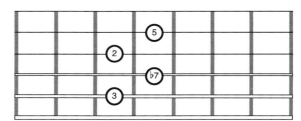

13th

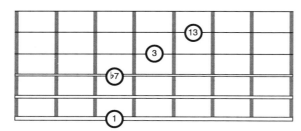

b7th

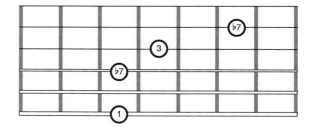

Dominant 7th - Lydian-Dominant - E-string Melody

E7#11

Root

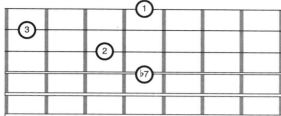

Root

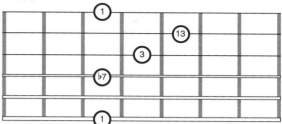

9th

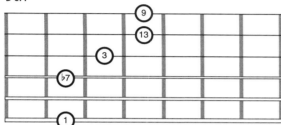

3rd

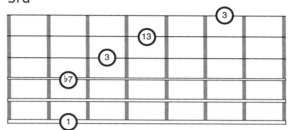

3rd

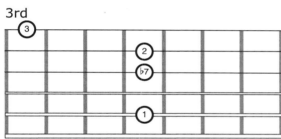

#4th

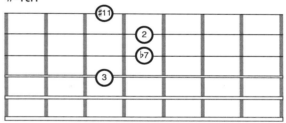

5th

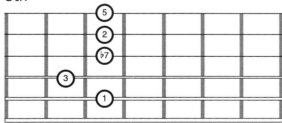

13th

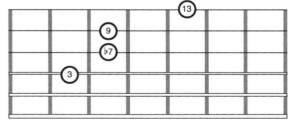

b7th

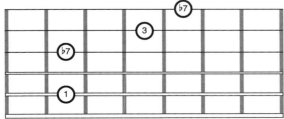

b7th

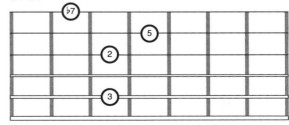

Mixolydian (Modal V) - B-string Melody   E7sus, E9sus, E13sus

Root

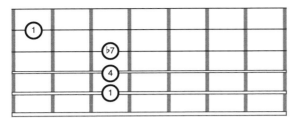

9th

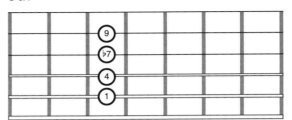

3rd

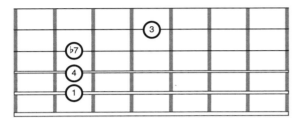

4th

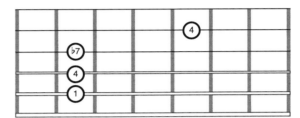

4th

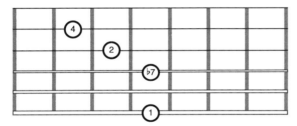

5th

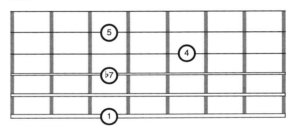

13th

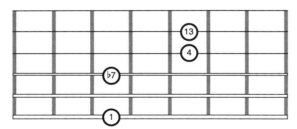

b7th

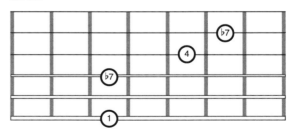

Root

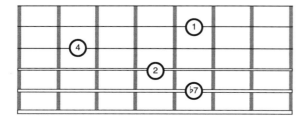

3rd

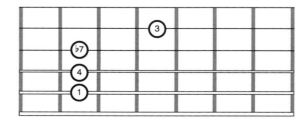

Mixolydian (Modal V) - E-string Melody   E7sus, E9sus, E13sus

Root

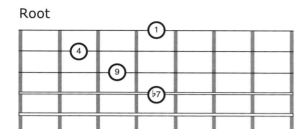

Root

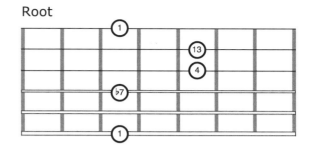

9th

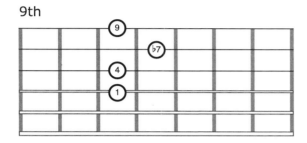

3rd

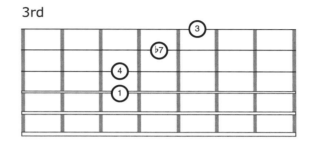

4th

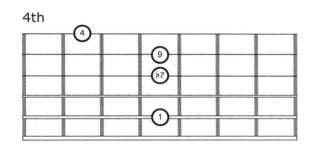

5th

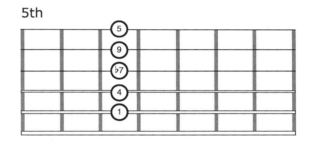

5th

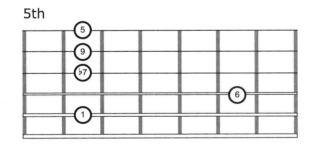

13th

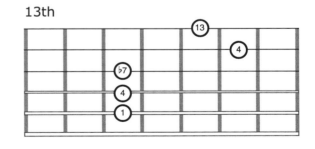

b7

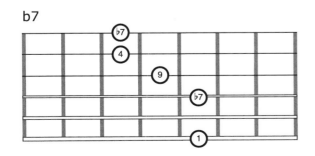

I. F Major (Ionian)

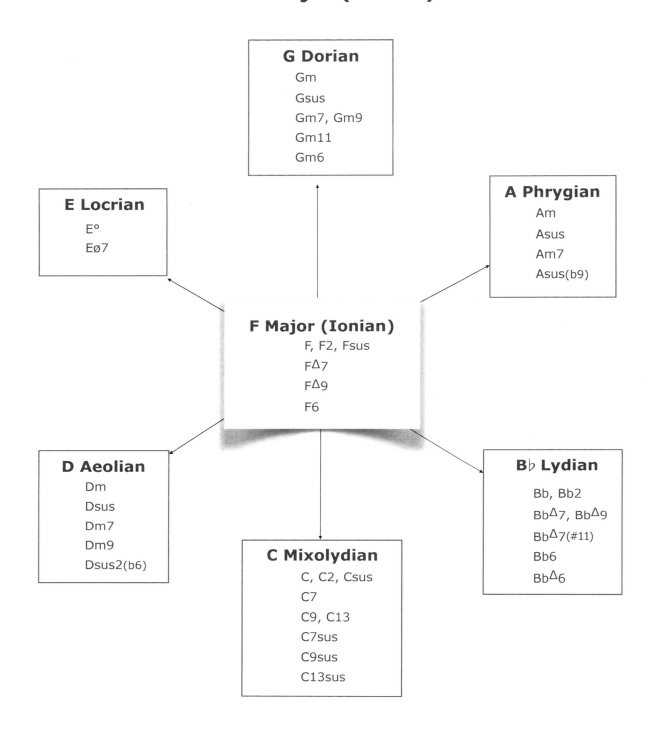

G Dorian
Gm
Gsus
Gm7, Gm9
Gm11
Gm6

A Phrygian
Am
Asus
Am7
Asus(b9)

E Locrian
E°
Eø7

F Major (Ionian)
F, F2, Fsus
FΔ7
FΔ9
F6

Bb Lydian
Bb, Bb2
BbΔ7, BbΔ9
BbΔ7(#11)
Bb6
BbΔ6

D Aeolian
Dm
Dsus
Dm7
Dm9
Dsus2(b6)

C Mixolydian
C, C2, Csus
C7
C9, C13
C7sus
C9sus
C13sus

F Major Scale - 7 Positions

FΔ7, FΔ9

F Major (Ionian)

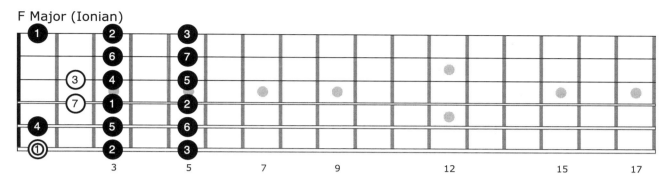

G Dorian

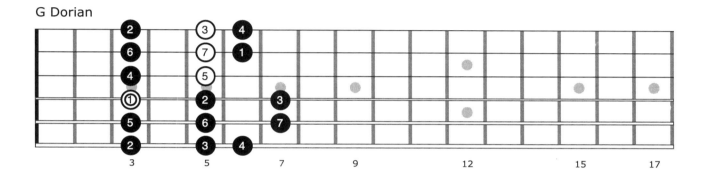

A Phrygian

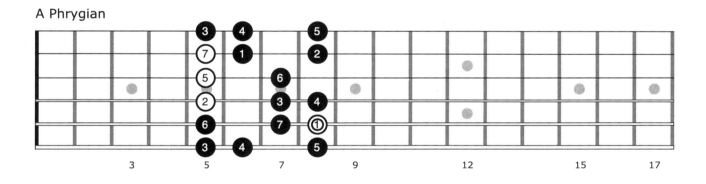

B♭ Lydian

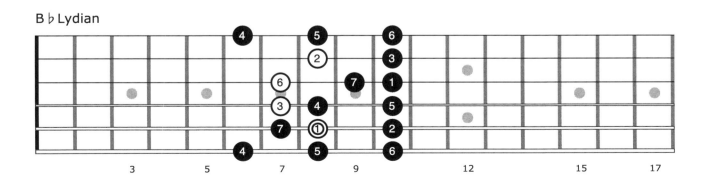

C Mixolydian

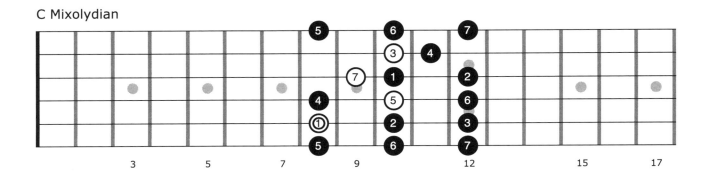

D Locrian

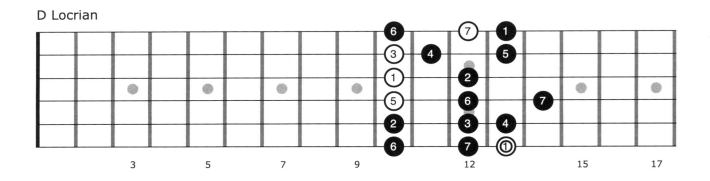

E Locrian

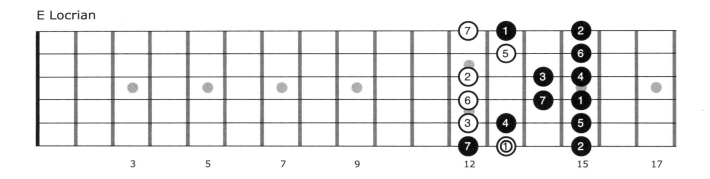

F Major (Ionian)

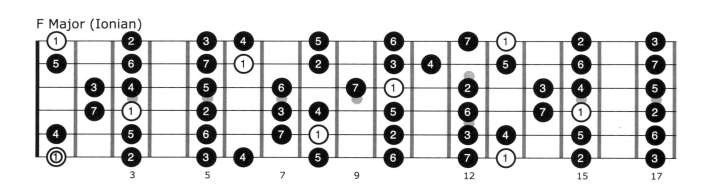

ii. F Dorian

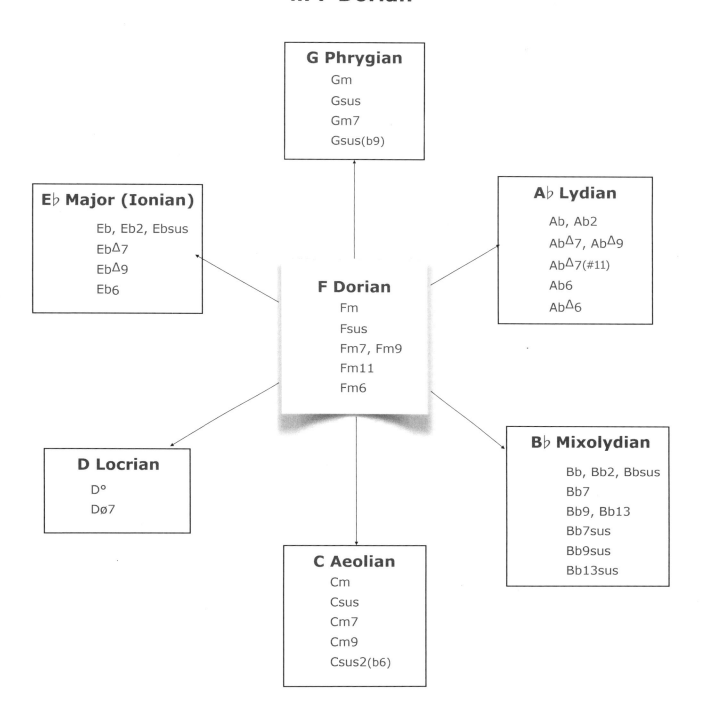

G Phrygian

Gm

Gsus

Gm7

Gsus(b9)

E♭ Major (Ionian)

Eb, Eb2, Ebsus

Eb$^\Delta$7

Eb$^\Delta$9

Eb6

A♭ Lydian

Ab, Ab2

Ab$^\Delta$7, Ab$^\Delta$9

Ab$^\Delta$7(#11)

Ab6

Ab$^\Delta$6

F Dorian

Fm

Fsus

Fm7, Fm9

Fm11

Fm6

D Locrian

D°

Dø7

B♭ Mixolydian

Bb, Bb2, Bbsus

Bb7

Bb9, Bb13

Bb7sus

Bb9sus

Bb13sus

C Aeolian

Cm

Csus

Cm7

Cm9

Csus2(b6)

F Dorian - 7 Positions

Fm7 / Fm9

F Dorian

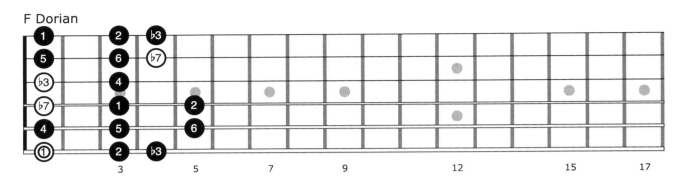

G Phrygian

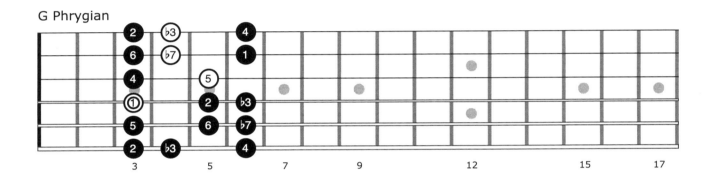

A♭ Lydian

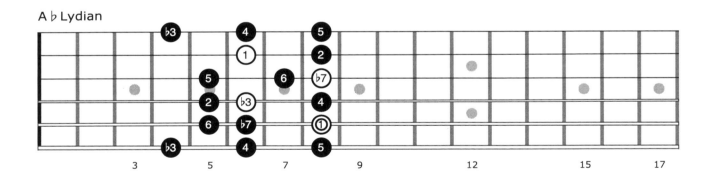

B♭ Mixolydian

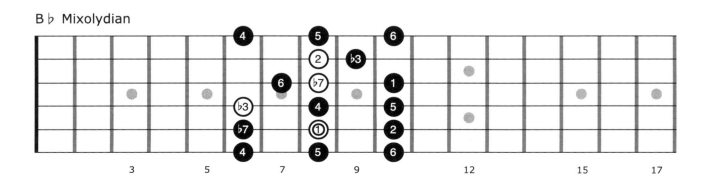

C Aeolian

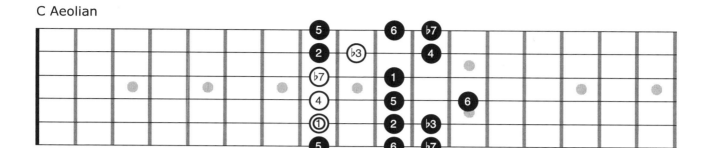

D Locrian

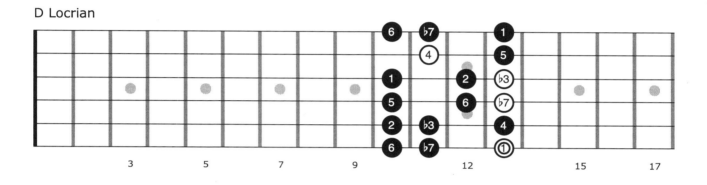

E♭ Major (Ionian)

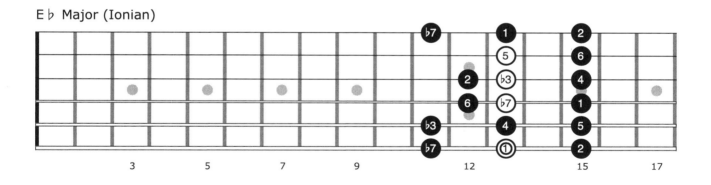

F Dorian

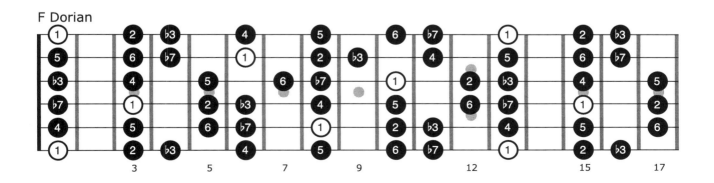

iii. F Phrygian

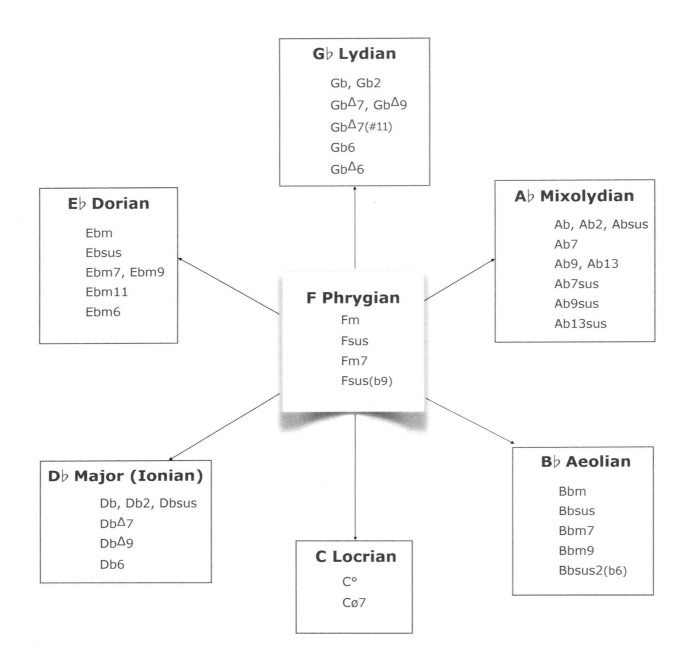

G♭ Lydian

Gb, Gb2
Gb△7, Gb△9
Gb△7(#11)
Gb6
Gb△6

E♭ Dorian

Ebm
Ebsus
Ebm7, Ebm9
Ebm11
Ebm6

A♭ Mixolydian

Ab, Ab2, Absus
Ab7
Ab9, Ab13
Ab7sus
Ab9sus
Ab13sus

F Phrygian

Fm
Fsus
Fm7
Fsus(b9)

D♭ Major (Ionian)

Db, Db2, Dbsus
Db△7
Db△9
Db6

C Locrian

C°
Cø7

B♭ Aeolian

Bbm
Bbsus
Bbm7
Bbm9
Bbsus2(b6)

F Phrygian - 7 Positions

Gsus(b9)

F Phrygian

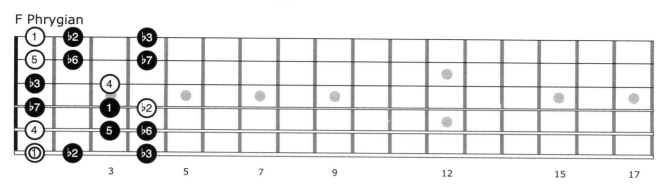

Gb Lydian

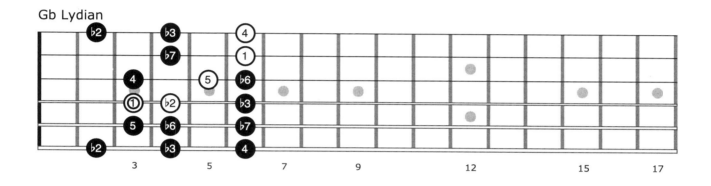

Ab Mixolydian

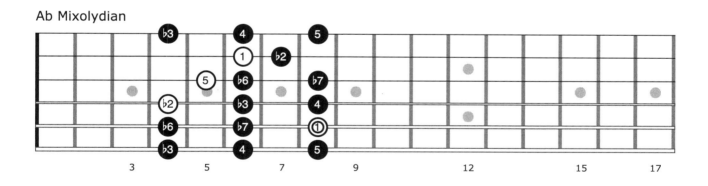

Bb Aeolian

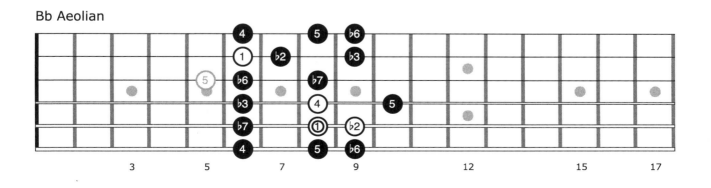

C Locrian

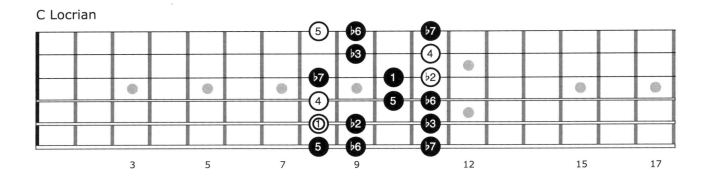

Db Major

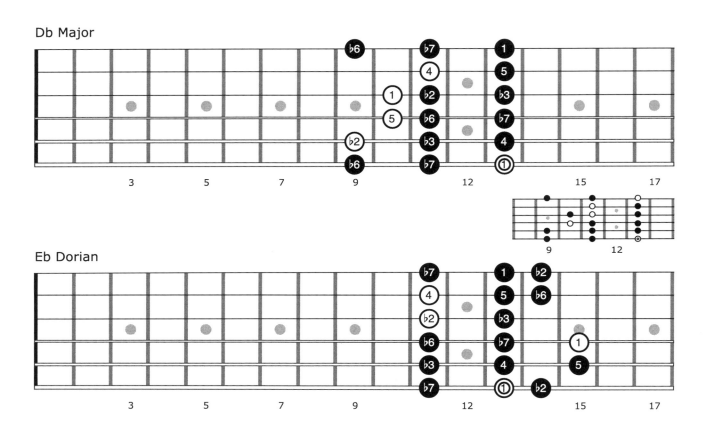

Eb Dorian

F Phrygian

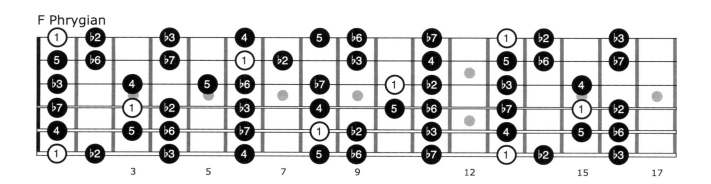

IV. F Lydian

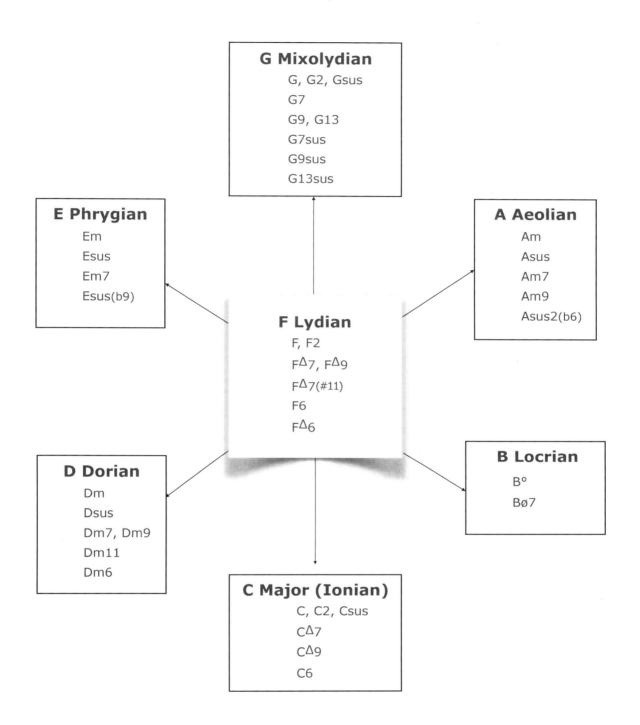

G Mixolydian

G, G2, Gsus

G7

G9, G13

G7sus

G9sus

G13sus

E Phrygian

Em

Esus

Em7

Esus(b9)

A Aeolian

Am

Asus

Am7

Am9

Asus2(b6)

F Lydian

F, F2

FΔ7, FΔ9

FΔ7(#11)

F6

FΔ6

D Dorian

Dm

Dsus

Dm7, Dm9

Dm11

Dm6

B Locrian

B°

Bø7

C Major (Ionian)

C, C2, Csus

CΔ7

CΔ9

C6

F Lydian - 7 Positions

FΔ7, FΔ7#11, FΔ9

F Lydian

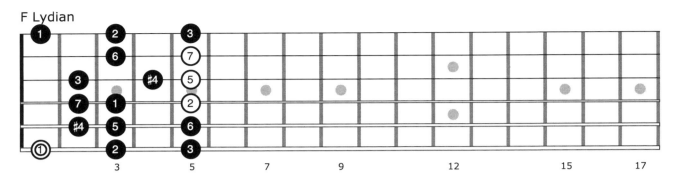

G Mixolydian

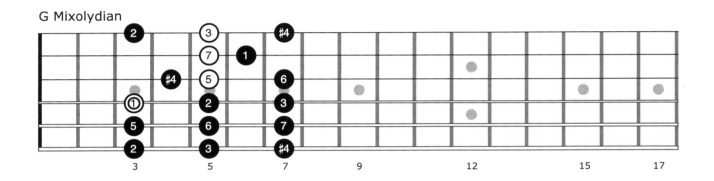

A Aeolian

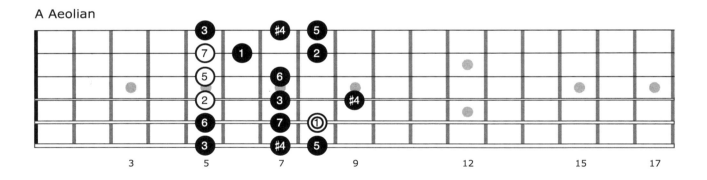

B Locrian

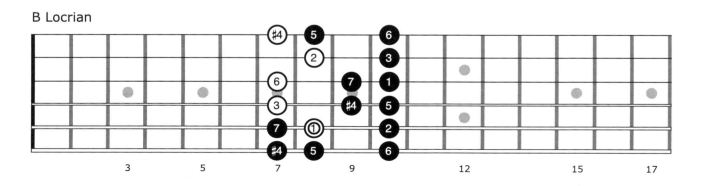

C Major (Ionian)

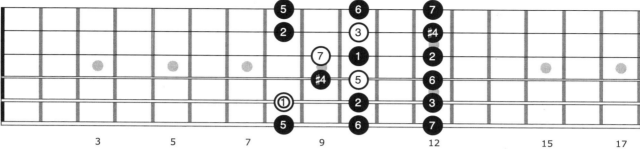

D Dorian

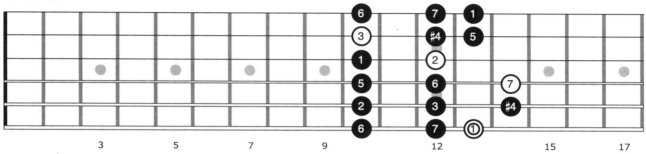

E Phrygian

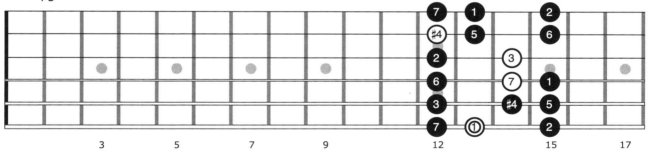

F Lydian

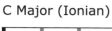

V. F Mixolydian

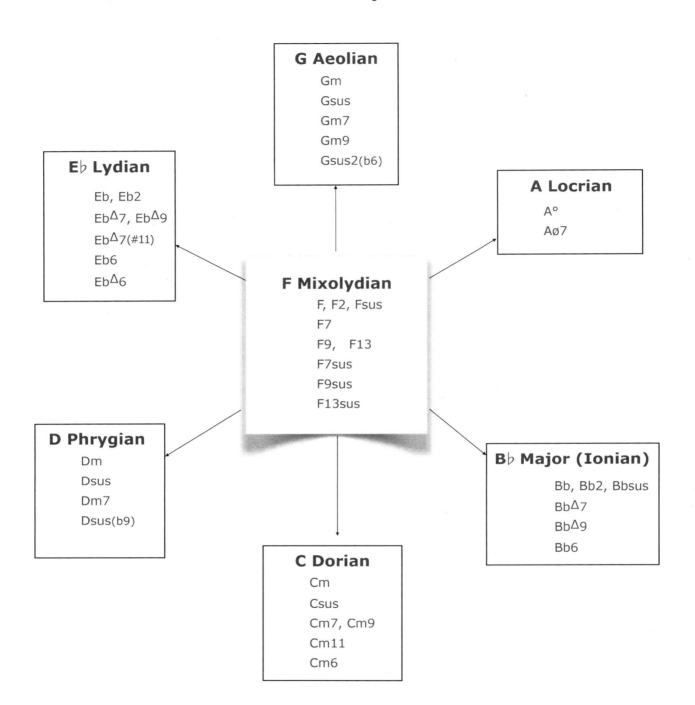

G Aeolian
Gm
Gsus
Gm7
Gm9
Gsus2(b6)

Eb Lydian
Eb, Eb2
Eb△7, Eb△9
Eb△7(#11)
Eb6
Eb△6

A Locrian
A°
Aø7

F Mixolydian
F, F2, Fsus
F7
F9, F13
F7sus
F9sus
F13sus

D Phrygian
Dm
Dsus
Dm7
Dsus(b9)

Bb Major (Ionian)
Bb, Bb2, Bbsus
Bb△7
Bb△9
Bb6

C Dorian
Cm
Csus
Cm7, Cm9
Cm11
Cm6

F Mixolydian - 7 Positions   F7

F Mixolydian

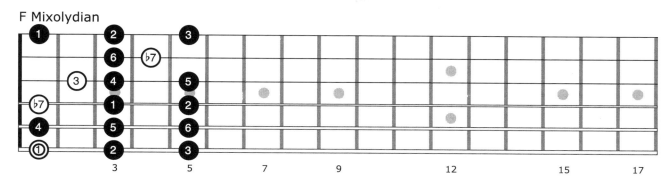

G Aeolian

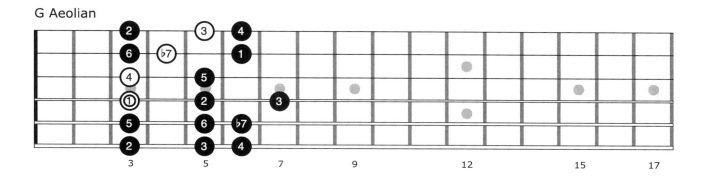

A Locrian

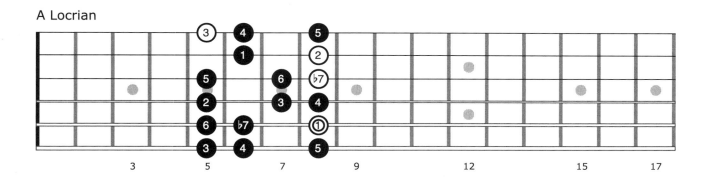

Bb Major (Ionian)

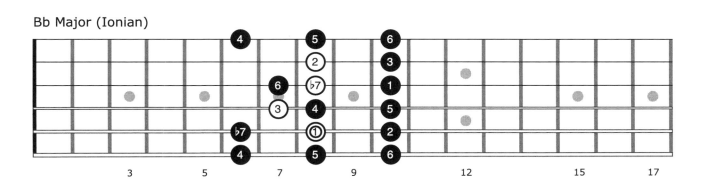

C Dorian

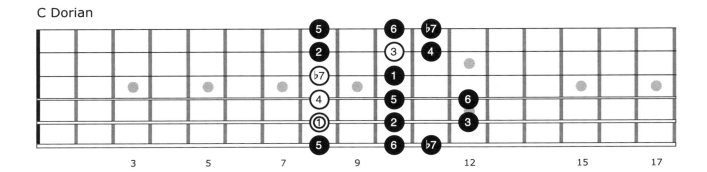

D Phrygian

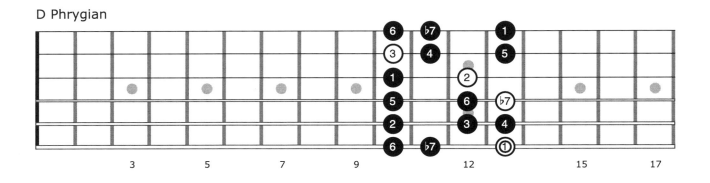

Eb Lydian

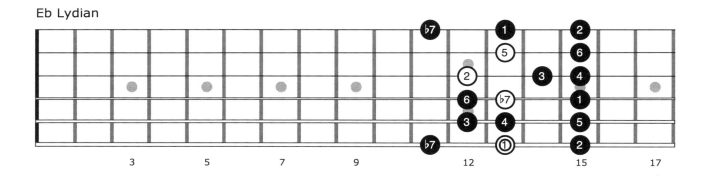

F Mixolydian

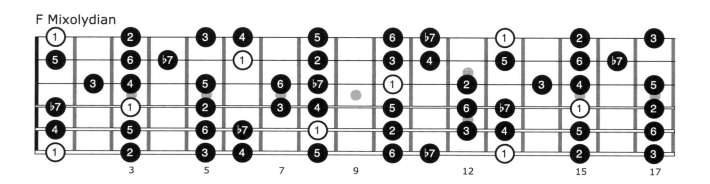

vi. F Aeolian

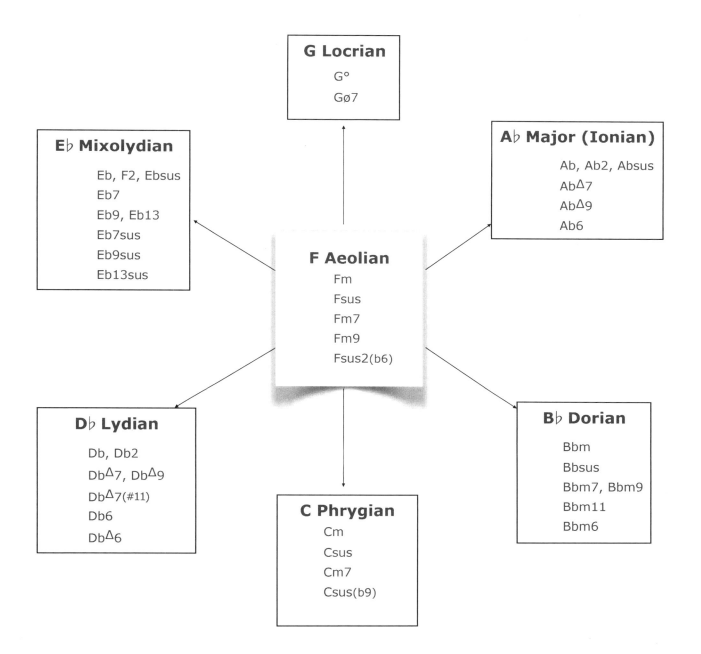

G Locrian

G°

Gø7

E♭ Mixolydian

Eb, F2, Ebsus

Eb7

Eb9, Eb13

Eb7sus

Eb9sus

Eb13sus

A♭ Major (Ionian)

Ab, Ab2, Absus

Ab△7

Ab△9

Ab6

F Aeolian

Fm

Fsus

Fm7

Fm9

Fsus2(b6)

D♭ Lydian

Db, Db2

Db△7, Db△9

Db△7(#11)

Db6

Db△6

B♭ Dorian

Bbm

Bbsus

Bbm7, Bbm9

Bbm11

Bbm6

C Phrygian

Cm

Csus

Cm7

Csus(b9)

87

F Aeolian - 7 Positions

Fm7

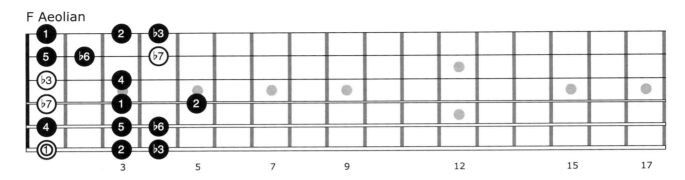

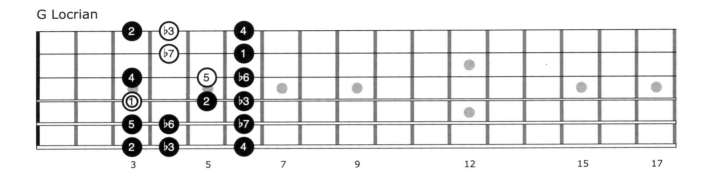

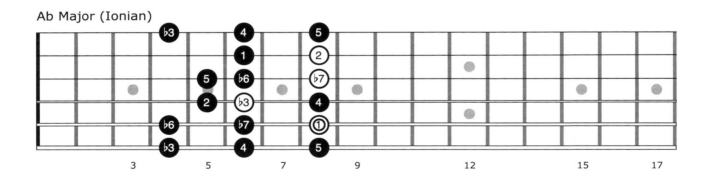

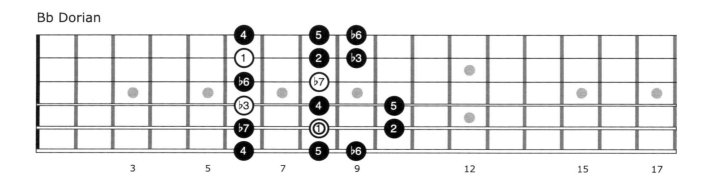

C Phrygian

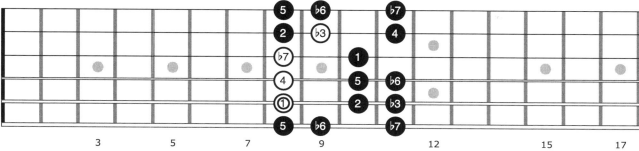

Db Lydian

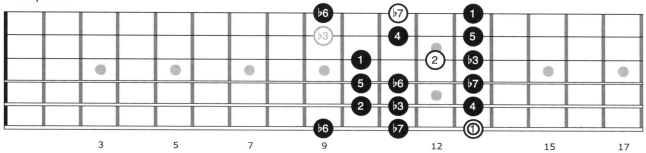

Eb Mixolydian

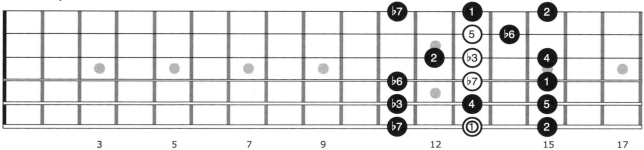

F Aeolian

vii. F Locrian

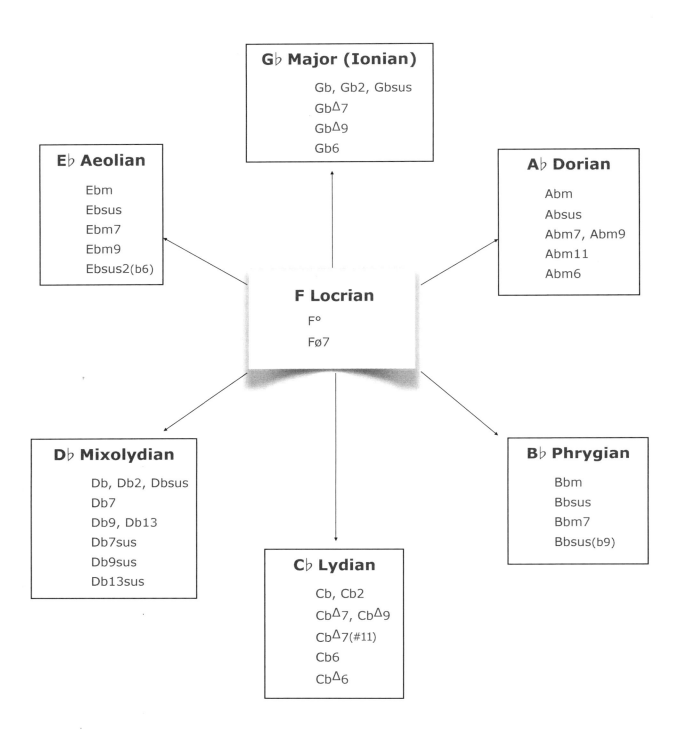

Gb Major (Ionian)

Gb, Gb2, Gbsus
Gb△7
Gb△9
Gb6

Eb Aeolian

Ebm
Ebsus
Ebm7
Ebm9
Ebsus2(b6)

Ab Dorian

Abm
Absus
Abm7, Abm9
Abm11
Abm6

F Locrian

F°
Fø7

Db Mixolydian

Db, Db2, Dbsus
Db7
Db9, Db13
Db7sus
Db9sus
Db13sus

Bb Phrygian

Bbm
Bbsus
Bbm7
Bbsus(b9)

Cb Lydian

Cb, Cb2
Cb△7, Cb△9
Cb△7(#11)
Cb6
Cb△6

F Locrian - 7 Positions

FØ7

F Locrian

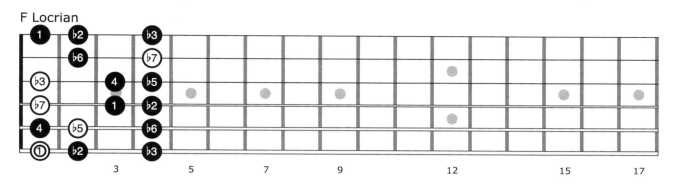

Gb Major (Ionian)

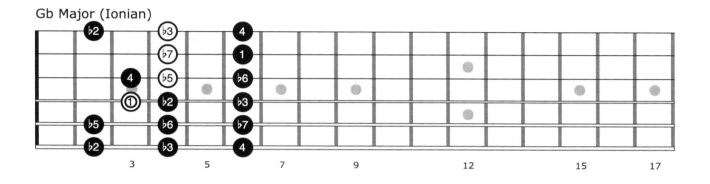

Ab Dorian

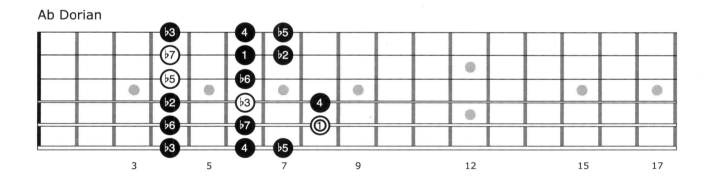

Bb Phrygian

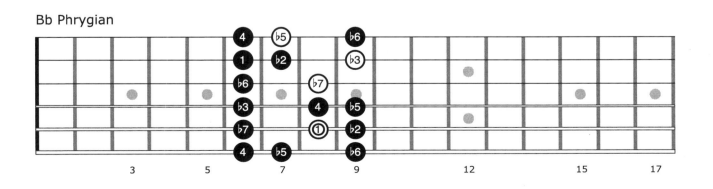

Cb Lydian

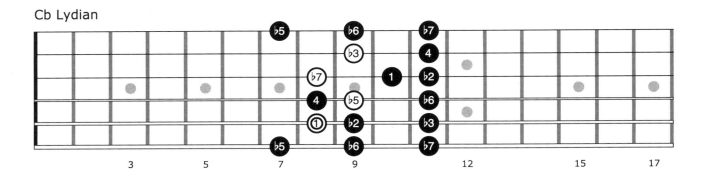

Db Mixolydian

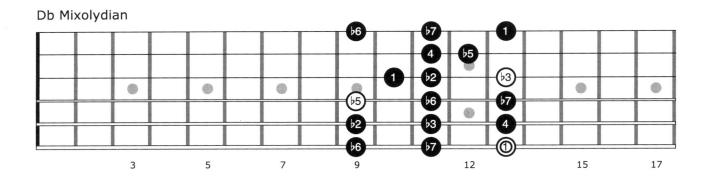

Eb Aeolian

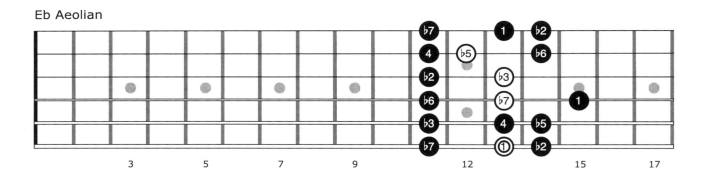

F Locrian

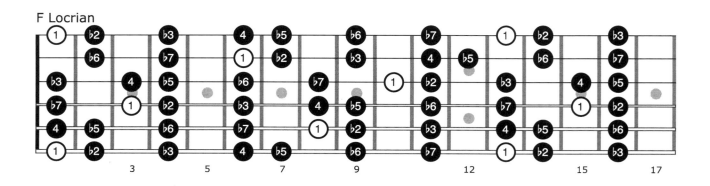

i. F Harmonic Minor

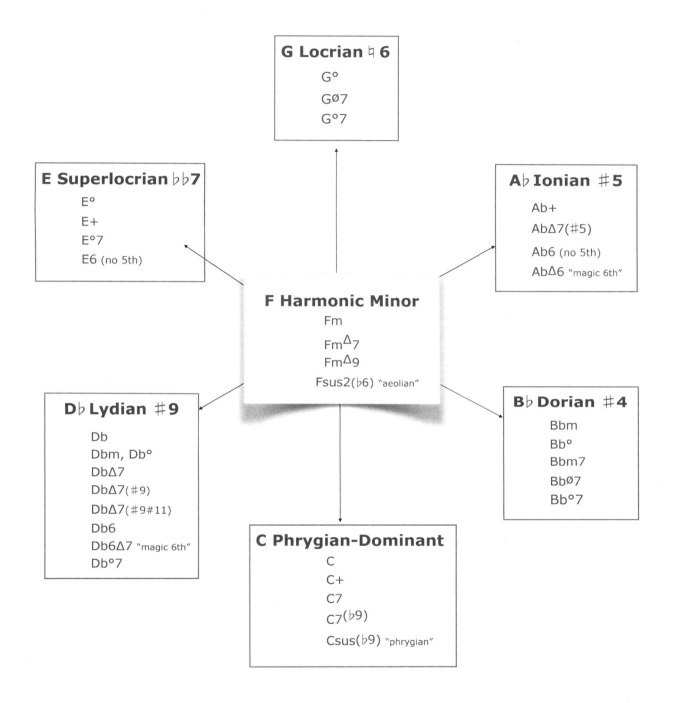

G Locrian ♮6
G°
Gø7
G°7

E Superlocrian ♭♭7
E°
E+
E°7
E6 (no 5th)

A♭ Ionian ♯5
Ab+
AbΔ7(♯5)
Ab6 (no 5th)
AbΔ6 "magic 6th"

F Harmonic Minor
Fm
Fm$^\Delta$7
Fm$^\Delta$9
Fsus2(♭6) "aeolian"

D♭ Lydian ♯9
Db
Dbm, Db°
DbΔ7
DbΔ7(♯9)
DbΔ7(♯9♯11)
Db6
Db6Δ7 "magic 6th"
Db°7

B♭ Dorian ♯4
Bbm
Bb°
Bbm7
Bbø7
Bb°7

C Phrygian-Dominant
C
C+
C7
C7(♭9)
Csus(♭9) "phrygian"

F Harmonic Minor - 7 Positions

FmΔ7, FmΔ9

F Harmonic Minor

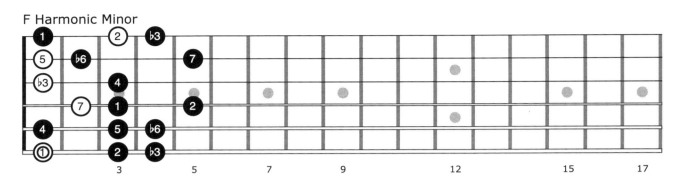

G Locrian ♮6

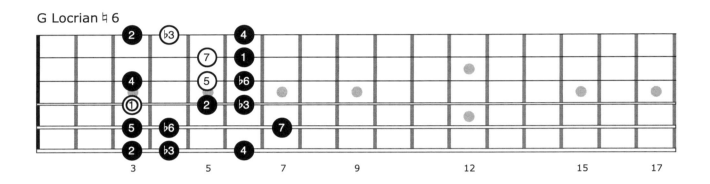

Ab Ionian #5

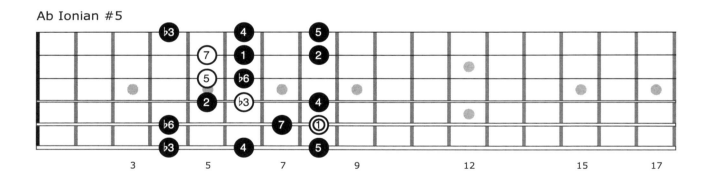

Bb Dorian #4

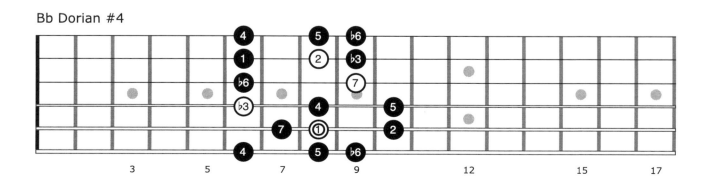

C Phrygian-Dominant

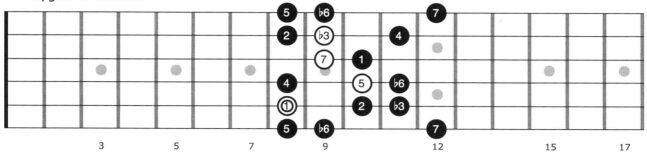

Db Lydian #9

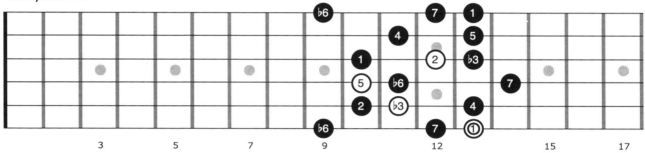

E Superlocrian bb7

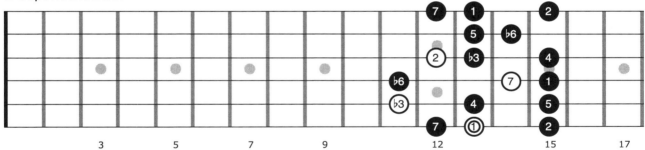

F Harmonic Minor

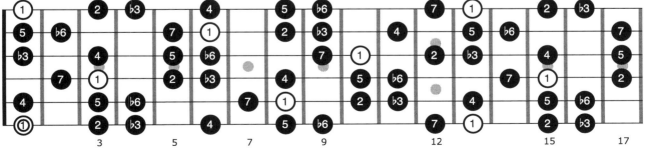

ii. F Locrian ♮6

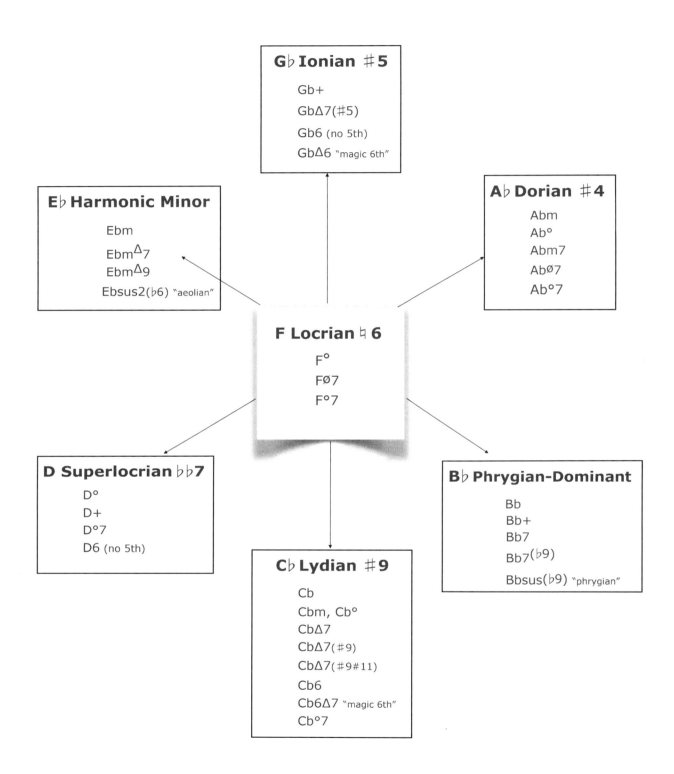

G♭ Ionian #5

Gb+

GbΔ7(#5)

Gb6 (no 5th)

GbΔ6 "magic 6th"

E♭ Harmonic Minor

Ebm

Ebm^Δ7

Ebm^Δ9

Ebsus2(♭6) "aeolian"

A♭ Dorian #4

Abm

Ab°

Abm7

AbØ7

Ab°7

F Locrian ♮6

F°

FØ7

F°7

D Superlocrian ♭♭7

D°

D+

D°7

D6 (no 5th)

B♭ Phrygian-Dominant

Bb

Bb+

Bb7

Bb7(♭9)

Bbsus(♭9) "phrygian"

C♭ Lydian #9

Cb

Cbm, Cb°

CbΔ7

CbΔ7(#9)

CbΔ7(#9#11)

Cb6

Cb6Δ7 "magic 6th"

Cb°7

96

F Locrian ♮6 - 7 Positions

Fø7

F Locrian ♮6

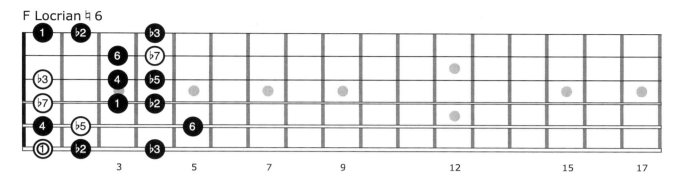

G♭ Ionian #5

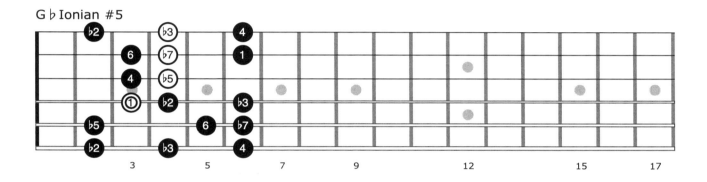

Ab Dorian #4

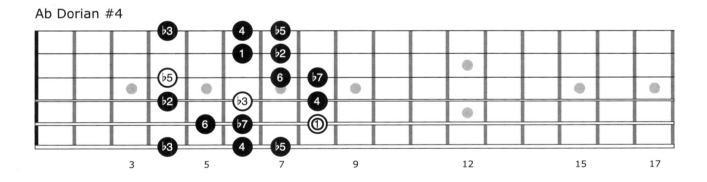

Bb Phrygian-Dominant

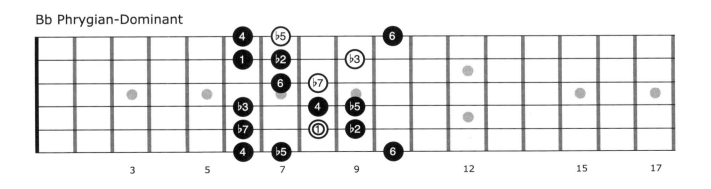

Cb Lydian #9

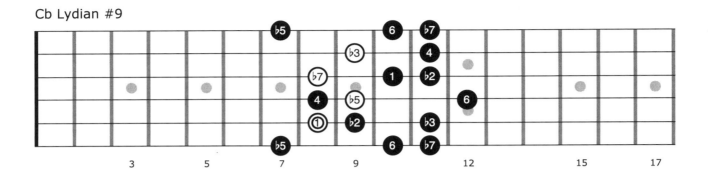

D Superlocrian bb7

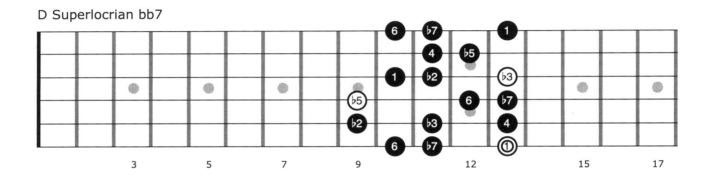

Eb Harmonic Minor

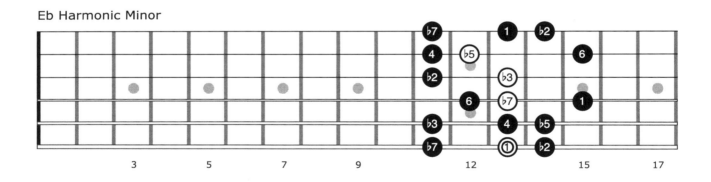

F Locrian ♮6

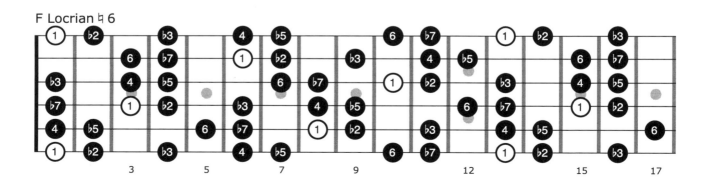

III. F Ionian ♯5

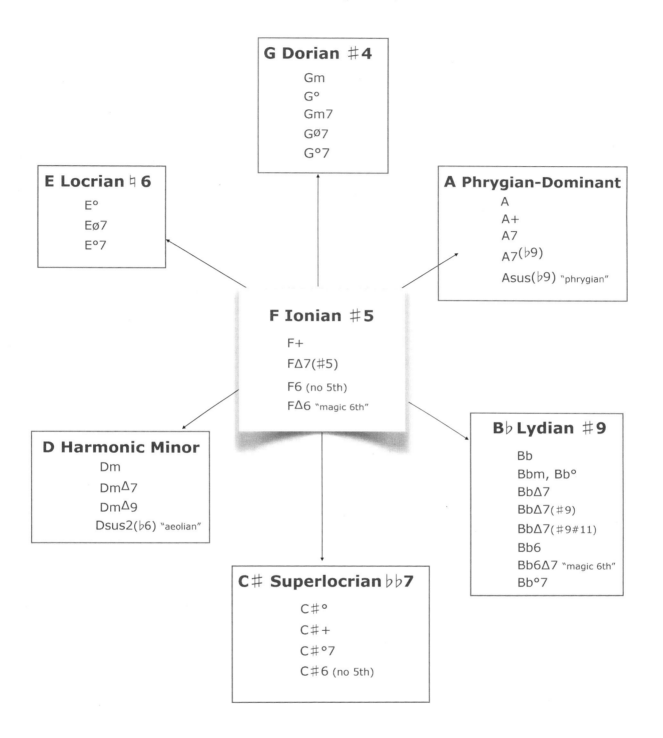

G Dorian ♯4

Gm
G°
Gm7
Gø7
G°7

E Locrian ♮6

E°
Eø7
E°7

A Phrygian-Dominant

A
A+
A7
A7(♭9)
Asus(♭9) "phrygian"

F Ionian ♯5

F+
FΔ7(♯5)
F6 (no 5th)
FΔ6 "magic 6th"

D Harmonic Minor

Dm
DmΔ7
DmΔ9
Dsus2(♭6) "aeolian"

B♭ Lydian ♯9

Bb
Bbm, Bb°
BbΔ7
BbΔ7(♯9)
BbΔ7(♯9♯11)
Bb6
Bb6Δ7 "magic 6th"
Bb°7

C♯ Superlocrian ♭♭7

C♯°
C♯+
C♯°7
C♯6 (no 5th)

F Ionian #5 - 7 Positions

FΔ7(♯5)

F Ionian #5

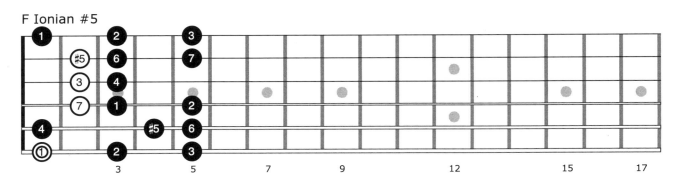

G Dorian #4

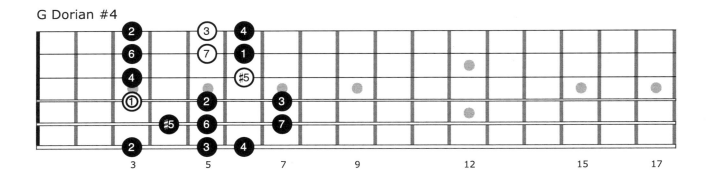

A Phrygian-Dominant

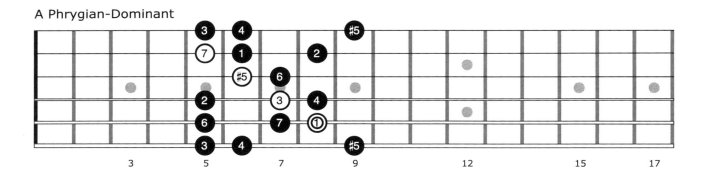

Bb Lydian #9

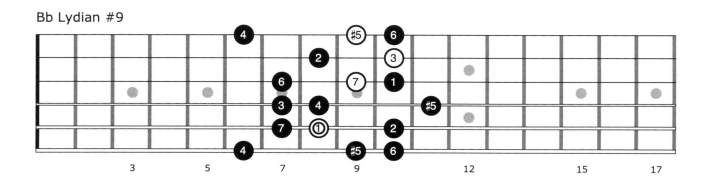

C# Superlocrian bb7

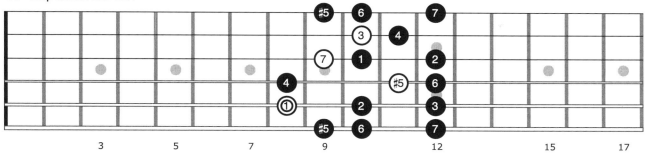

D Harmonic Minor

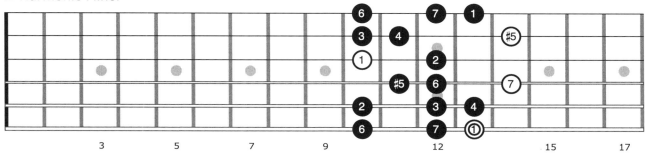

E Locrian ♮6

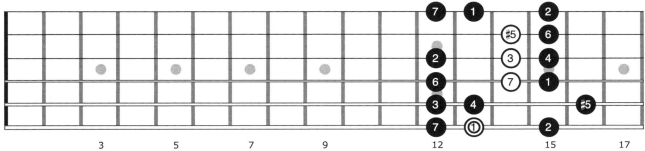

F Ionian #5

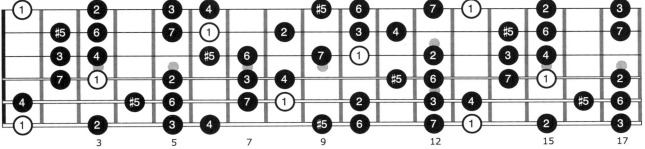

iv. F Dorian ♯4

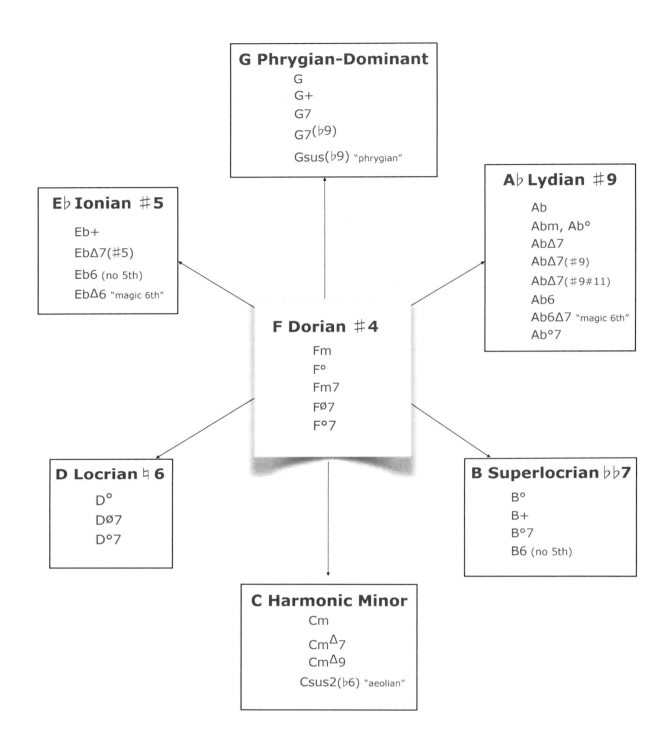

G Phrygian-Dominant
G
G+
G7
G7(♭9)
Gsus(♭9) "phrygian"

E♭ Ionian ♯5
Eb+
EbΔ7(♯5)
Eb6 (no 5th)
EbΔ6 "magic 6th"

A♭ Lydian ♯9
Ab
Abm, Ab°
AbΔ7
AbΔ7(♯9)
AbΔ7(♯9♯11)
Ab6
Ab6Δ7 "magic 6th"
Ab°7

F Dorian ♯4
Fm
F°
Fm7
FØ7
F°7

D Locrian ♮6
D°
DØ7
D°7

B Superlocrian ♭♭7
B°
B+
B°7
B6 (no 5th)

C Harmonic Minor
Cm
CmΔ7
CmΔ9
Csus2(♭6) "aeolian"

F Dorian #4 - 7 Positions

Fm7

F Dorian #4

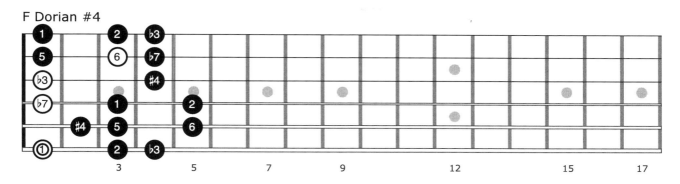

G Phrygian-Dominant

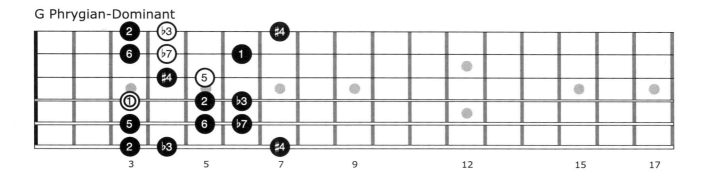

Ab Lydian #9

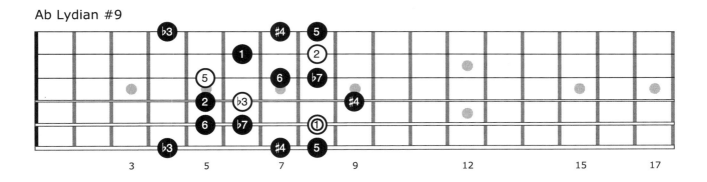

B Superlocrian bb7

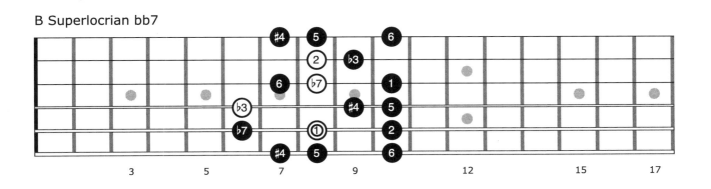

C Harmonic Minor

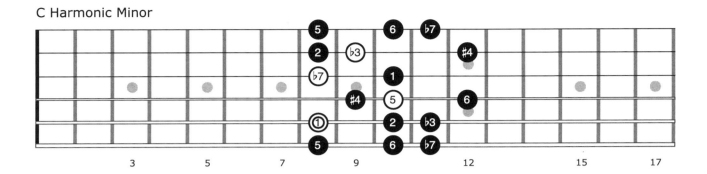

D Locrian ♮6

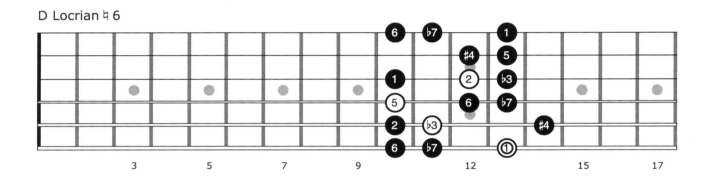

Eb Ionian #5

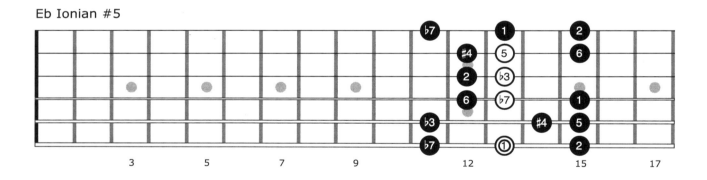

F Dorian #4

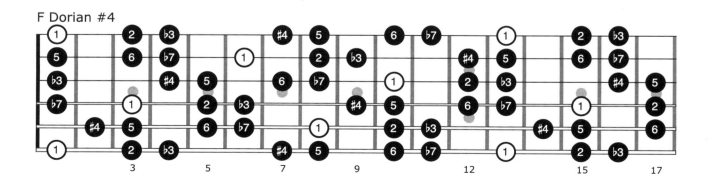

V. F Phrygian-Dominant

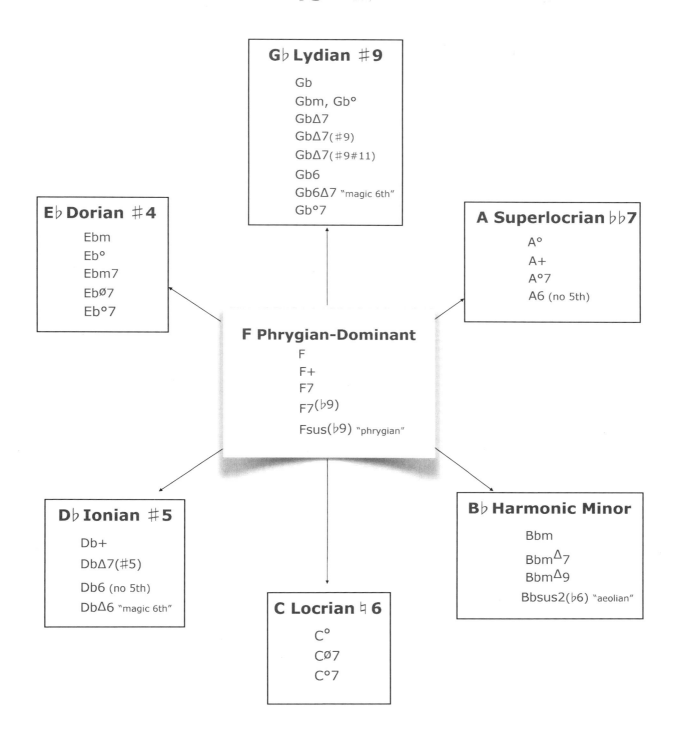

Gb Lydian ♯9

Gb
Gbm, Gb°
GbΔ7
GbΔ7(♯9)
GbΔ7(♯9♯11)
Gb6
Gb6Δ7 "magic 6th"
Gb°7

Eb Dorian ♯4

Ebm
Eb°
Ebm7
EbØ7
Eb°7

A Superlocrian ♭♭7

A°
A+
A°7
A6 (no 5th)

F Phrygian-Dominant

F
F+
F7
F7(♭9)
Fsus(♭9) "phrygian"

Db Ionian ♯5

Db+
DbΔ7(♯5)
Db6 (no 5th)
DbΔ6 "magic 6th"

C Locrian ♮6

C°
CØ7
C°7

Bb Harmonic Minor

Bbm
BbmΔ7
BbmΔ9
Bbsus2(♭6) "aeolian"

F Phrygian-Dominant - 7 Positions   F7

F Phrygian-Dominant

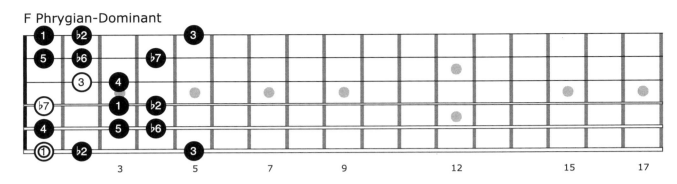

Gb Lydian #9

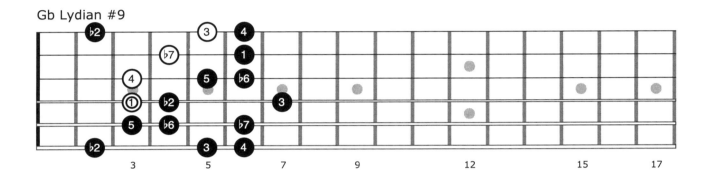

A Superlocrian bb7

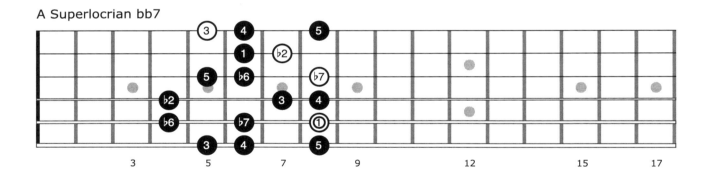

Bb Harmonic Minor

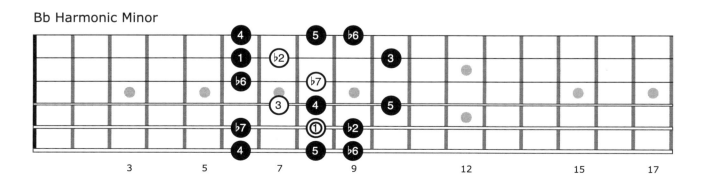

C Locrian ♮6

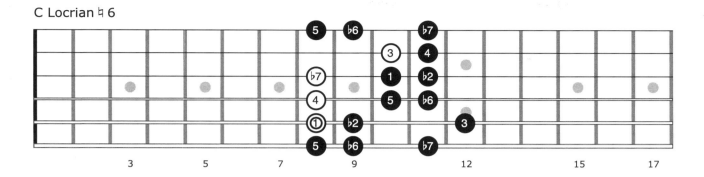

Db Ionian #5

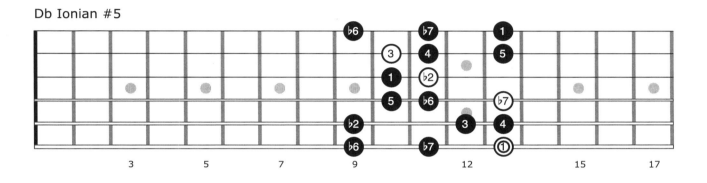

Eb Dorian #4

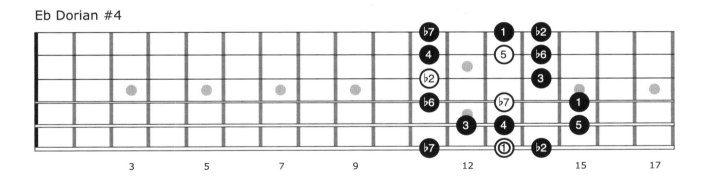

F Phrygian-Dominant

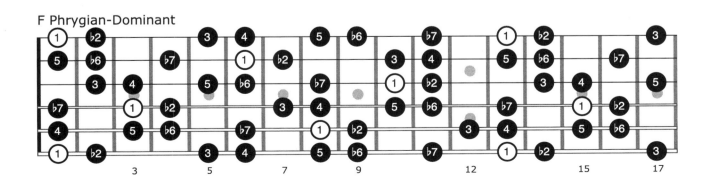

VI. F Lydian ♯9

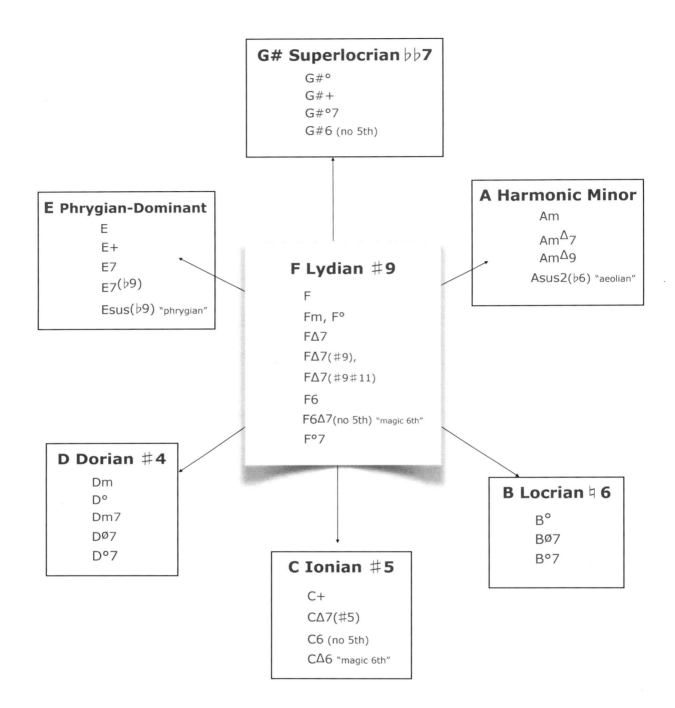

G♯ Superlocrian ♭♭7

G♯°
G♯+
G♯°7
G♯6 (no 5th)

E Phrygian-Dominant

E
E+
E7
E7(♭9)
Esus(♭9) "phrygian"

A Harmonic Minor

Am
Am△7
Am△9
Asus2(♭6) "aeolian"

F Lydian ♯9

F
Fm, F°
F△7
F△7(♯9),
F△7(♯9♯11)
F6
F6△7(no 5th) "magic 6th"
F°7

D Dorian ♯4

Dm
D°
Dm7
DØ7
D°7

B Locrian ♮6

B°
BØ7
B°7

C Ionian ♯5

C+
C△7(♯5)
C6 (no 5th)
C△6 "magic 6th"

F Lydian #9 - 7 Positions

FΔ7

F Lydian #9 - FΔ7

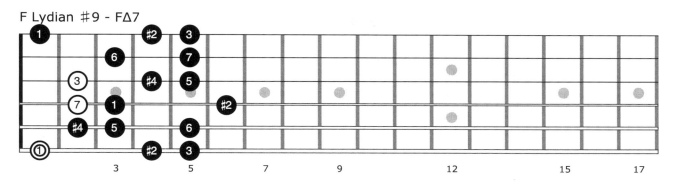

G Superlocrian bb7

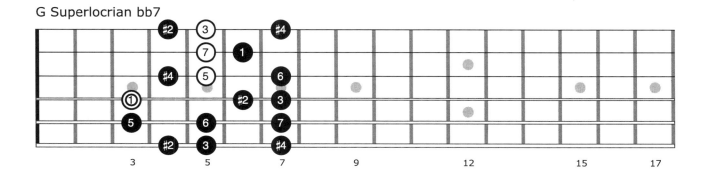

Ab Harmonic Minor

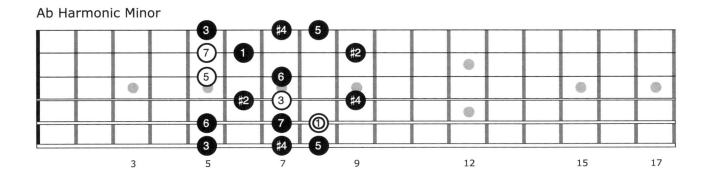

Bb Locrian ♮6

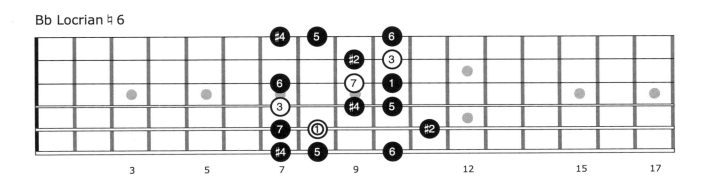

C Ionian #5

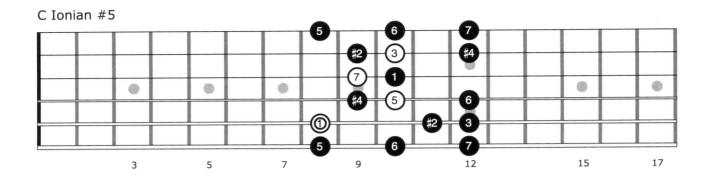

D Dorian #4

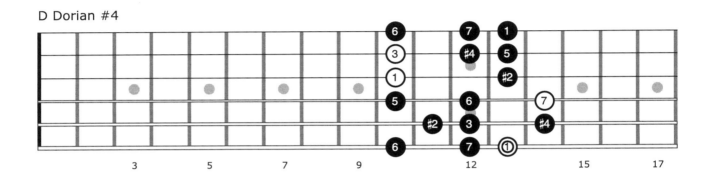

E Phrygian-Dominant

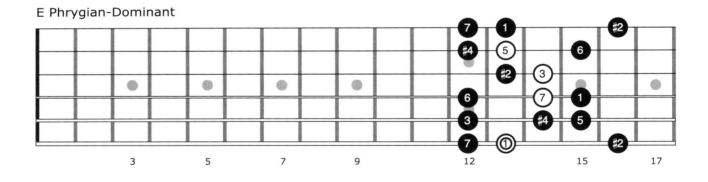

F Lydian #9

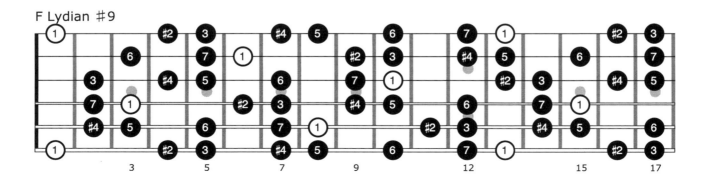

vii. G Superlocrian ♭♭7

(G "Ultralocrian"/Altered ♭♭7)

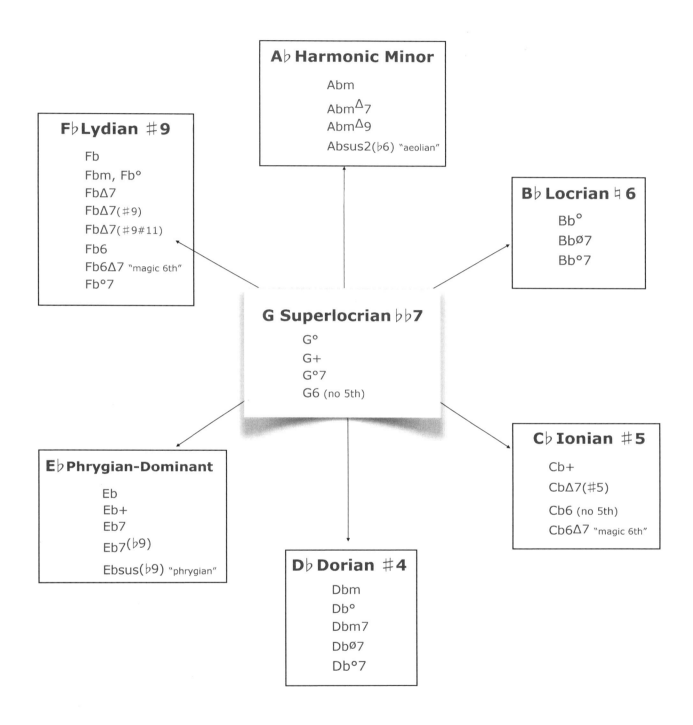

A♭ Harmonic Minor

Abm

Abm△7

Abm△9

Absus2(♭6) "aeolian"

F♭ Lydian ♯9

Fb

Fbm, Fb°

Fb△7

Fb△7(♯9)

Fb△7(♯9♯11)

Fb6

Fb6△7 "magic 6th"

Fb°7

B♭ Locrian ♮6

Bb°

BbØ7

Bb°7

G Superlocrian ♭♭7

G°

G+

G°7

G6 (no 5th)

E♭ Phrygian-Dominant

Eb

Eb+

Eb7

Eb7(♭9)

Ebsus(♭9) "phrygian"

C♭ Ionian ♯5

Cb+

Cb△7(♯5)

Cb6 (no 5th)

Cb6△7 "magic 6th"

D♭ Dorian ♯4

Dbm

Db°

Dbm7

DbØ7

Db°7

G Superlocrian bb7 - 7 Positions

G°7

G Superlocrian bb7

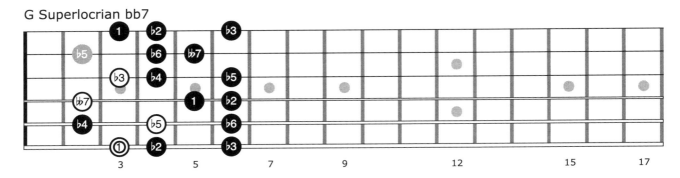

Ab Harmonic Minor

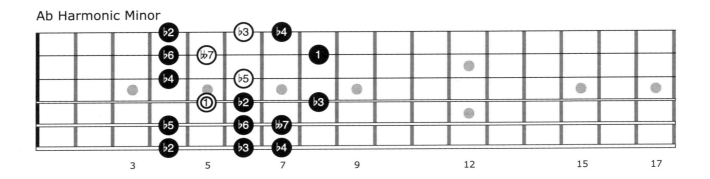

Bb Locrian ♮6

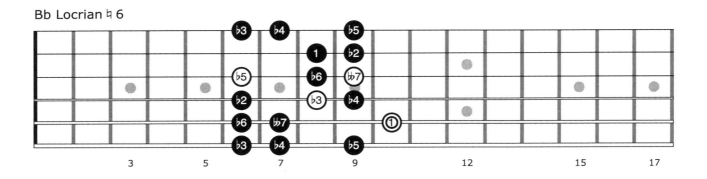

Cb Ionian #5

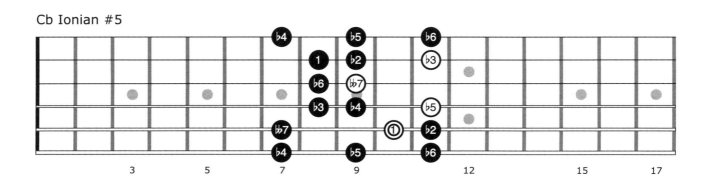

Db Dorian #4

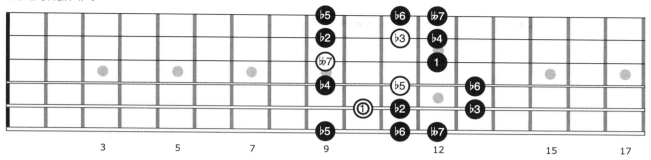

Eb Phrygian-Dominant

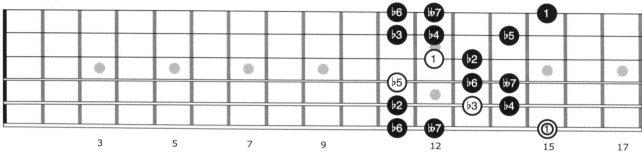

Fb Lydian #9

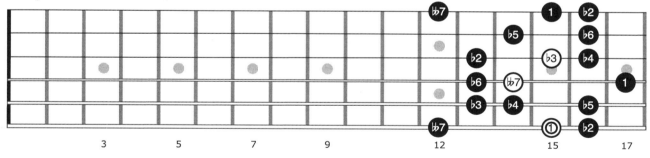

G Superlocrian bb7

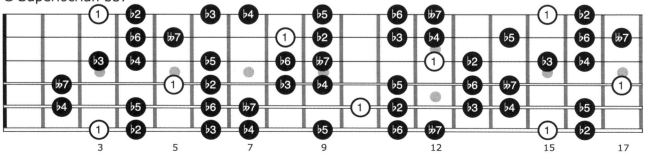

i. F Melodic Minor

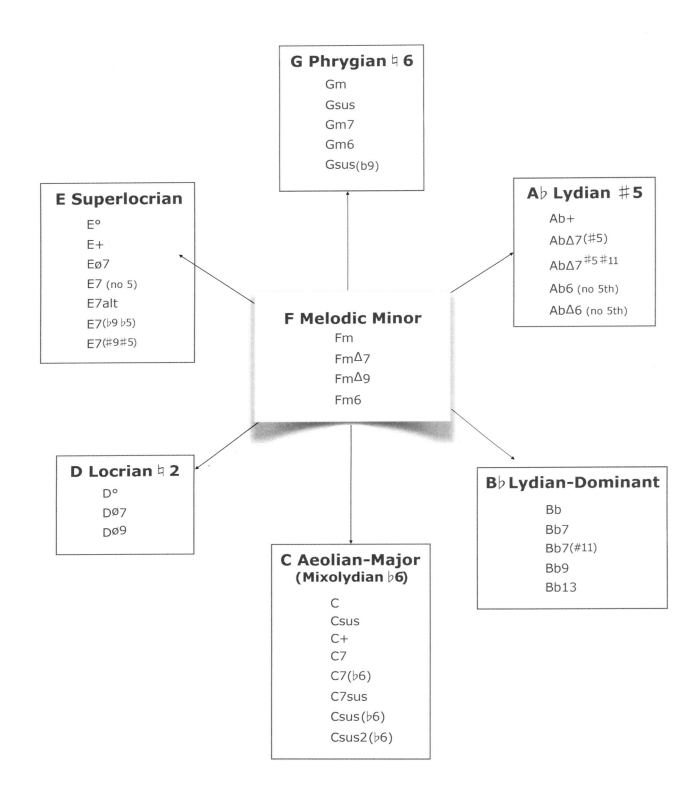

G Phrygian ♮6

Gm
Gsus
Gm7
Gm6
Gsus(b9)

E Superlocrian

E°
E+
Eø7
E7 (no 5)
E7alt
E7(b9 b5)
E7(#9#5)

A♭ Lydian ♯5

Ab+
AbΔ7(♯5)
AbΔ7 ♯5 ♯11
Ab6 (no 5th)
AbΔ6 (no 5th)

F Melodic Minor

Fm
FmΔ7
FmΔ9
Fm6

D Locrian ♮2

D°
Dø7
Dø9

C Aeolian-Major
(Mixolydian ♭6)

C
Csus
C+
C7
C7(b6)
C7sus
Csus(b6)
Csus2(b6)

B♭ Lydian-Dominant

Bb
Bb7
Bb7(#11)
Bb9
Bb13

F Melodic Minor - 7 Positions

FmΔ7, FmΔ9

F Melodic Minor

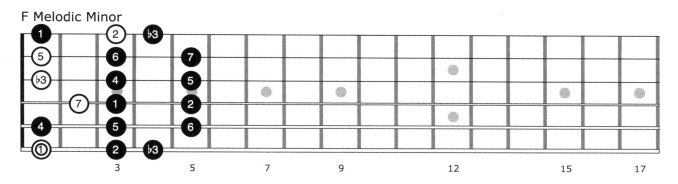

G Phrygian ♮6/Dorian ♭2

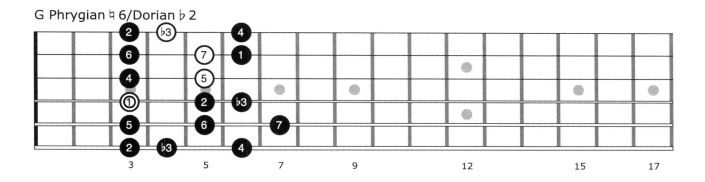

A♭ Lydian-Augmented

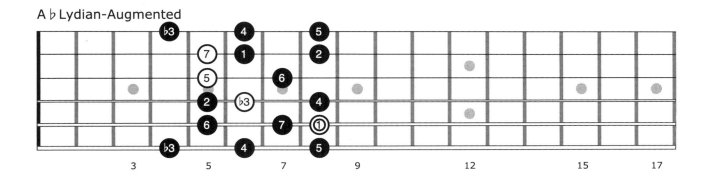

B♭ Lydian-Dominant

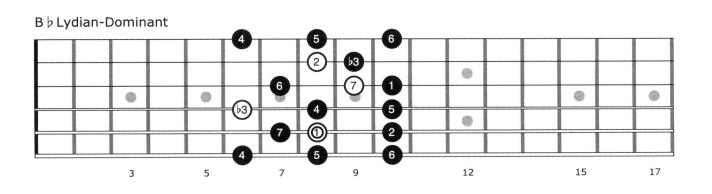

C Aeolian-Major/Mixolydian ♭6

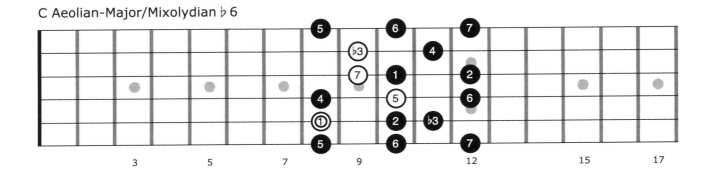

D Locrian ♮2

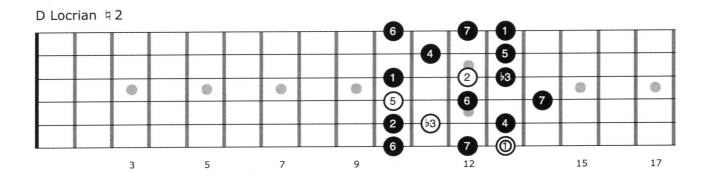

E Superlocrian/Altered

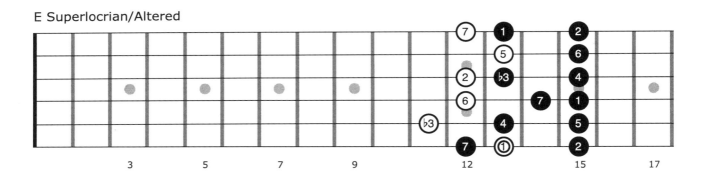

F Melodic Minor / Ionian b3

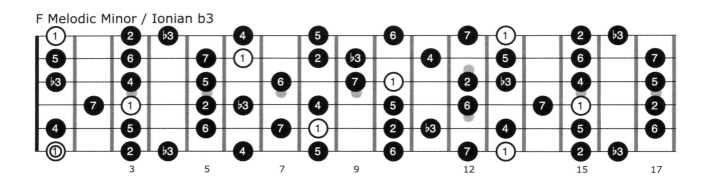

ii. F Phrygian ♮6

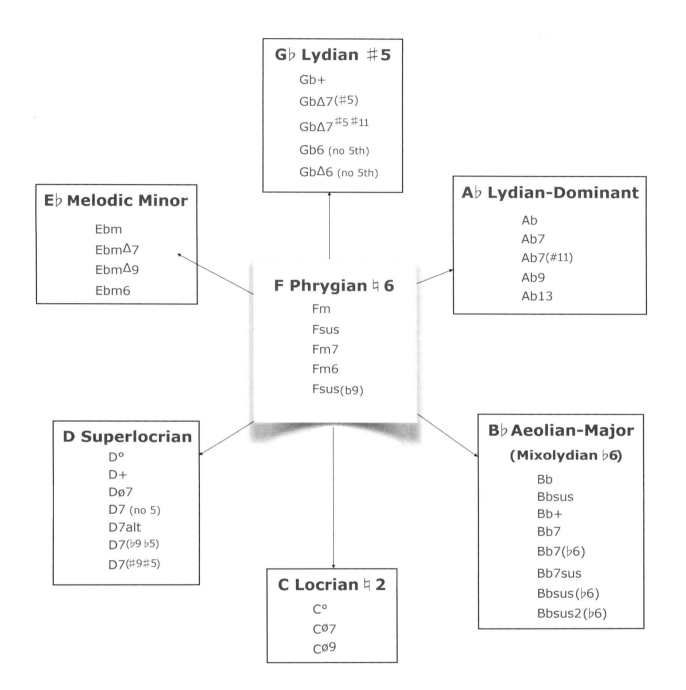

G♭ Lydian ♯5

Gb+

GbΔ7(♯5)

GbΔ7 ♯5 ♯11

Gb6 (no 5th)

GbΔ6 (no 5th)

E♭ Melodic Minor

Ebm

EbmΔ7

EbmΔ9

Ebm6

A♭ Lydian-Dominant

Ab

Ab7

Ab7(♯11)

Ab9

Ab13

F Phrygian ♮6

Fm

Fsus

Fm7

Fm6

Fsus(b9)

D Superlocrian

D°

D+

Dø7

D7 (no 5)

D7alt

D7(♭9 ♭5)

D7(♯9♯5)

B♭ Aeolian-Major

(Mixolydian ♭6)

Bb

Bbsus

Bb+

Bb7

Bb7(♭6)

Bb7sus

Bbsus(♭6)

Bbsus2(♭6)

C Locrian ♮2

C°

Cø7

Cø9

F Phrygian ♮6/Dorian ♭2 - 7 Positions

Fsus(b9)

F Phrygian ♮6/Dorian ♭2

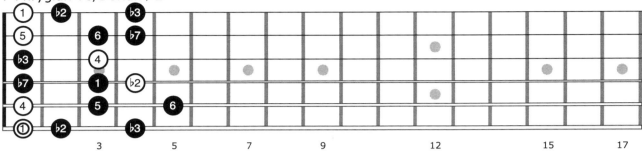

G♭ Lydian-Augmented

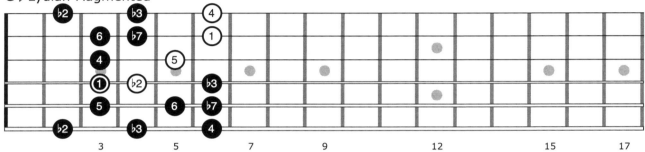

A♭ Lydian-Dominant

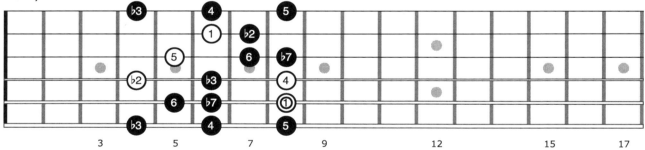

B♭ Aeolian-Major/Mixolydian ♭6

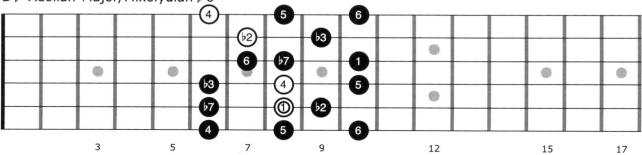

C Locrian ♮2

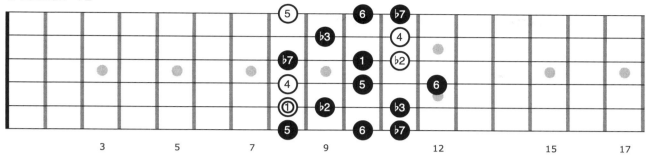

D Superlocrian/Altered

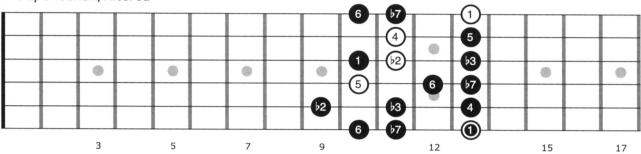

E♭ Melodic Minor

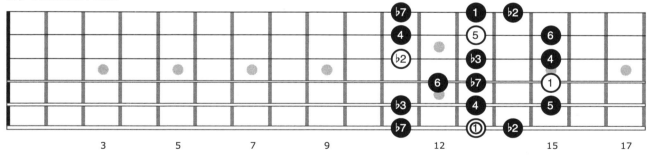

F Phrygian ♮6/Dorian ♭2

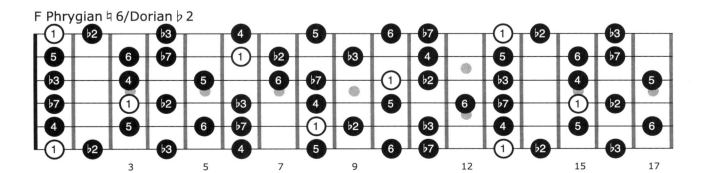

III. F Lydian ♯5

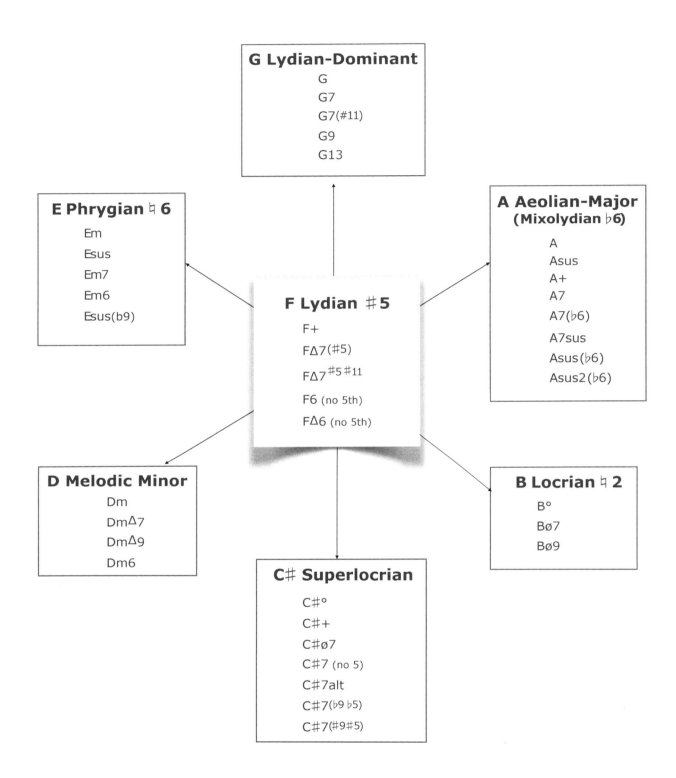

G Lydian-Dominant
G
G7
G7(♯11)
G9
G13

E Phrygian ♮6
Em
Esus
Em7
Em6
Esus(b9)

A Aeolian-Major
(Mixolydian ♭6)
A
Asus
A+
A7
A7(♭6)
A7sus
Asus(♭6)
Asus2(♭6)

F Lydian ♯5
F+
FΔ7(♯5)
FΔ7 ♯5 ♯11
F6 (no 5th)
FΔ6 (no 5th)

D Melodic Minor
Dm
DmΔ7
DmΔ9
Dm6

B Locrian ♮2
B°
Bø7
Bø9

C♯ Superlocrian
C♯°
C♯+
C♯ø7
C♯7 (no 5)
C♯7alt
C♯7(♭9 ♭5)
C♯7(♯9♯5)

F Lydian-Augmented - 7 Positions FΔ7(♯5)

F Lydian-Augmented

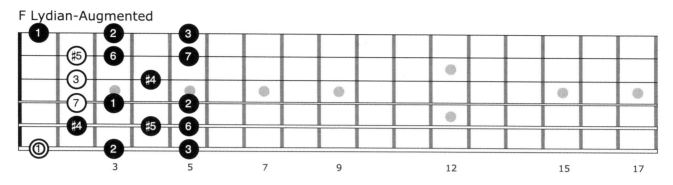

G Lydian-Dominant

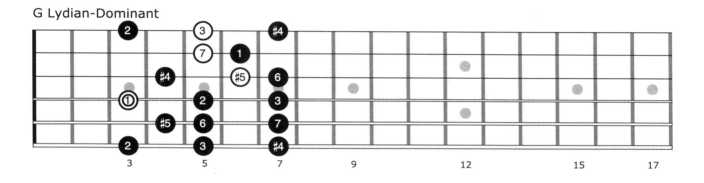

A Aeolian-Major/Mixolydian ♭6

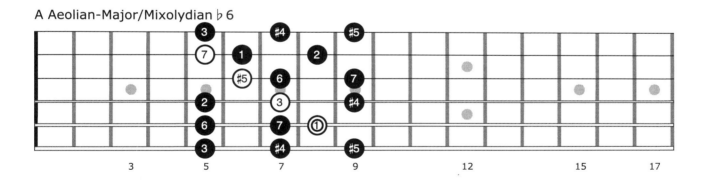

B Locrian ♮2

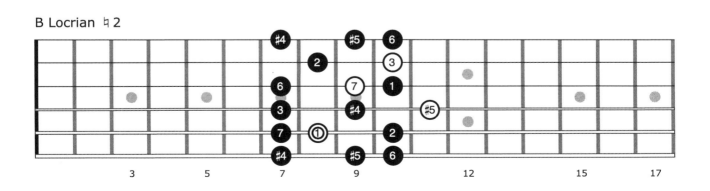

121

C# Superlocrian/Altered

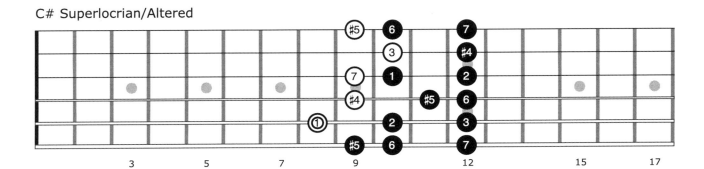

D Melodic Minor

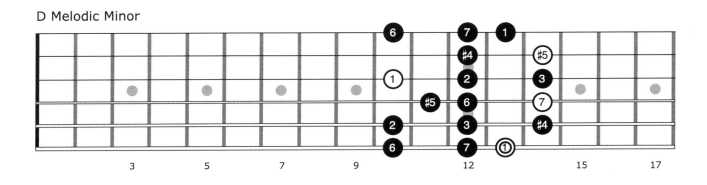

E Phrygian ♮6/Dorian ♭2

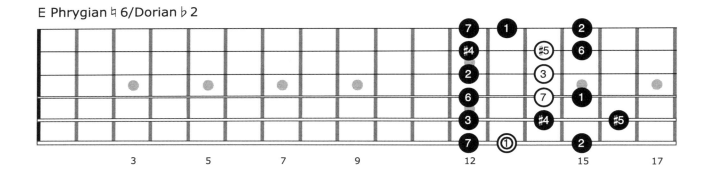

F Lydian #5 (Augmented)

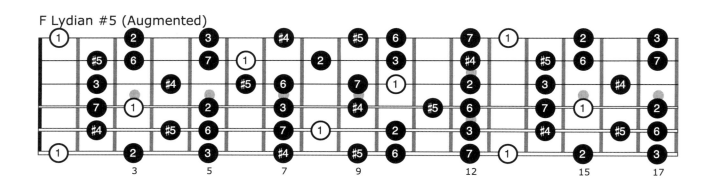

IV. F Lydian-Dominant

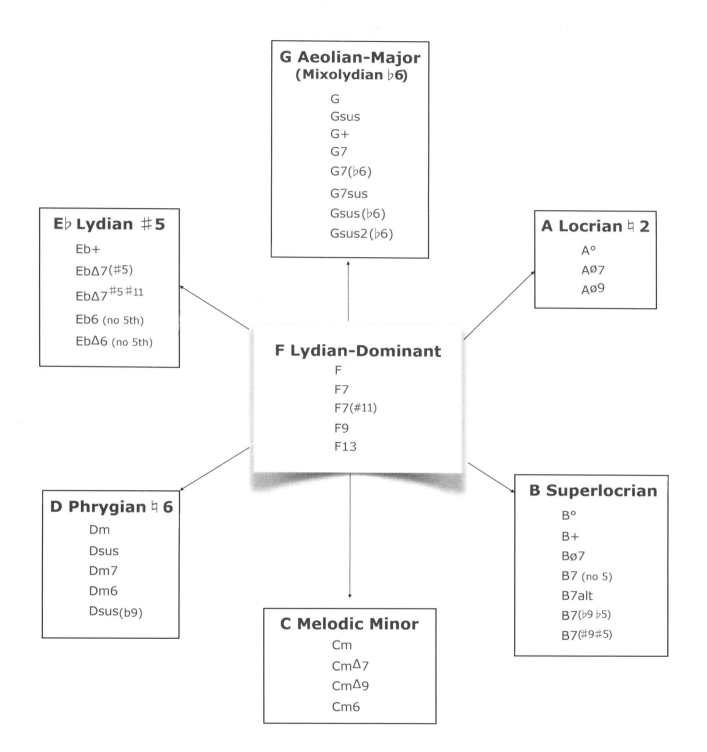

G Aeolian-Major
(Mixolydian ♭6)

G
Gsus
G+
G7
G7(♭6)
G7sus
Gsus(♭6)
Gsus2(♭6)

E♭ Lydian #5

Eb+
EbΔ7(#5)
EbΔ7 #5 #11
Eb6 (no 5th)
EbΔ6 (no 5th)

A Locrian ♮2

A°
AØ7
AØ9

F Lydian-Dominant

F
F7
F7(#11)
F9
F13

D Phrygian ♮6

Dm
Dsus
Dm7
Dm6
Dsus(b9)

B Superlocrian

B°
B+
BØ7
B7 (no 5)
B7alt
B7(♭9 ♭5)
B7(#9#5)

C Melodic Minor

Cm
CmΔ7
CmΔ9
Cm6

F Lydian-Dominant - 7 Positions

F7, F7#11, F9, F13

F Lydian-Dominant

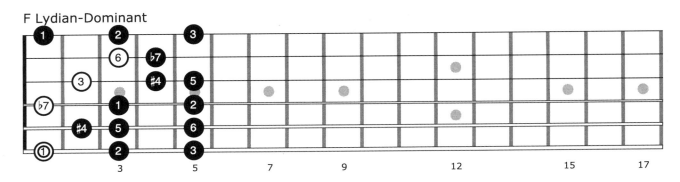

G Aeolian-Major/Mixolydian ♭6

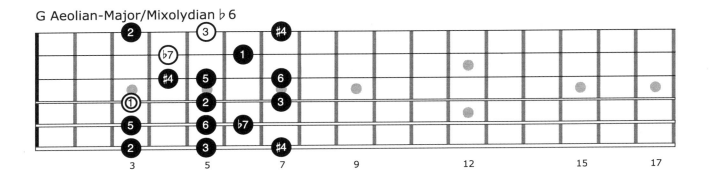

A Locrian ♮2

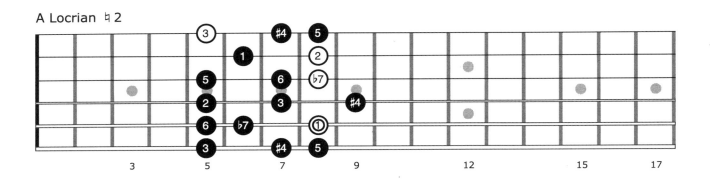

B Superlocrian/Altered

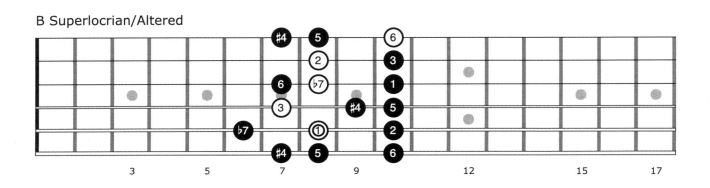

C Melodic Minor

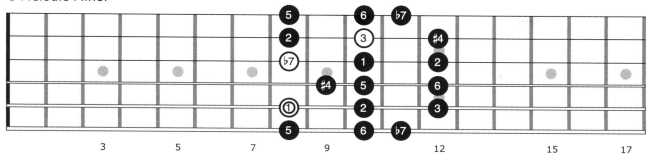

D Phrygian ♮6/Dorian ♭2

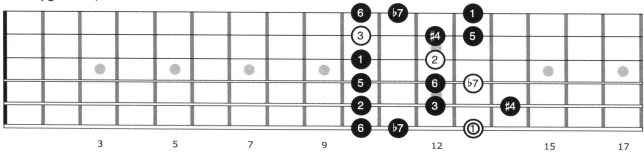

Eb Lydian-Augmented

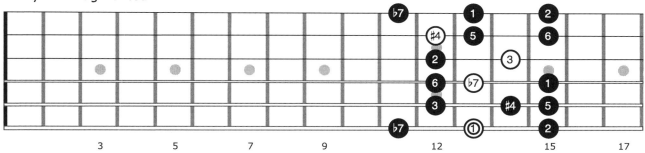

F Lydian-Dominant

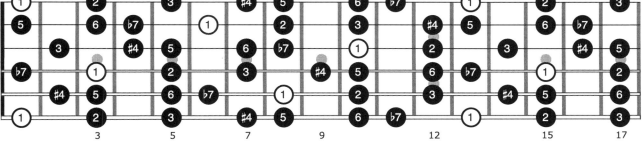

V. F Aeolian-Major
(F Mixolydian ♭6)

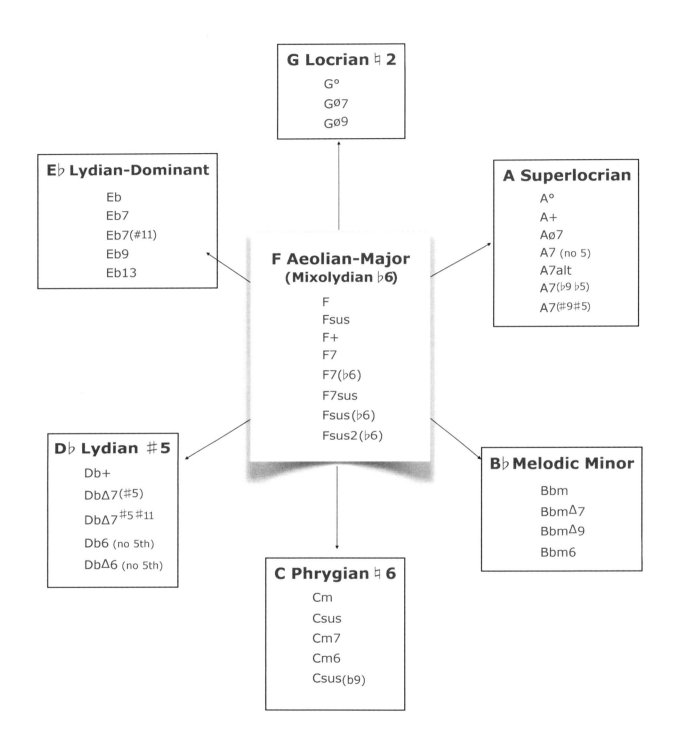

G Locrian ♮2

G°
Gø7
Gø9

E♭ Lydian-Dominant

Eb
Eb7
Eb7(#11)
Eb9
Eb13

A Superlocrian

A°
A+
Aø7
A7 (no 5)
A7alt
A7(♭9 ♭5)
A7(#9#5)

F Aeolian-Major
(Mixolydian ♭6)

F
Fsus
F+
F7
F7(♭6)
F7sus
Fsus(♭6)
Fsus2(♭6)

D♭ Lydian #5

Db+
DbΔ7(#5)
DbΔ7 #5 #11
Db6 (no 5th)
DbΔ6 (no 5th)

B♭ Melodic Minor

Bbm
BbmΔ7
BbmΔ9
Bbm6

C Phrygian ♮6

Cm
Csus
Cm7
Cm6
Csus(b9)

F Aeolian-Major/Mixolydian ♭6 - 7 Positions   F7

F Aeolian-Major (Mix b6) - G7

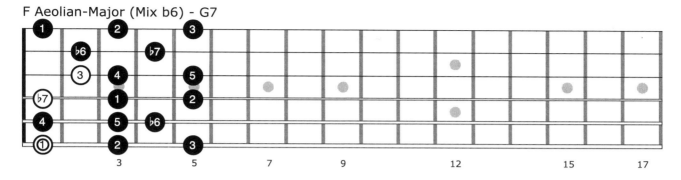

G Locrian ♮2

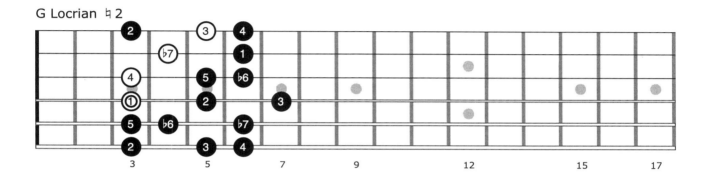

A Superlocrian/Altered

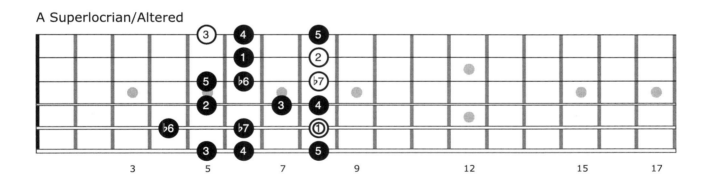

Bb Melodic Minor

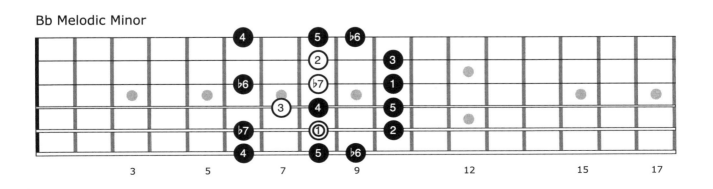

127

C Phrygian ♮6/Dorian ♭2

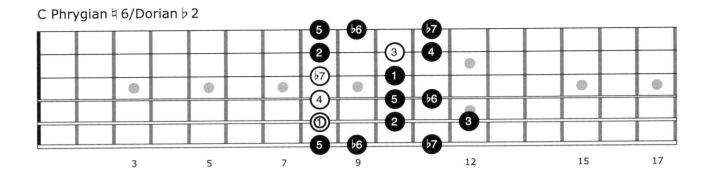

Db Lydian-Augmented

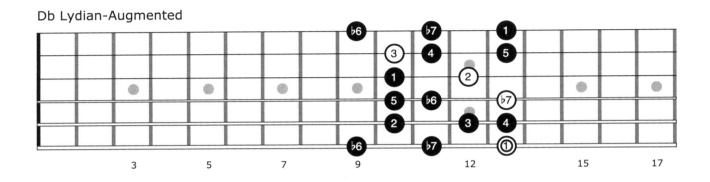

Eb Lydian-Dominant

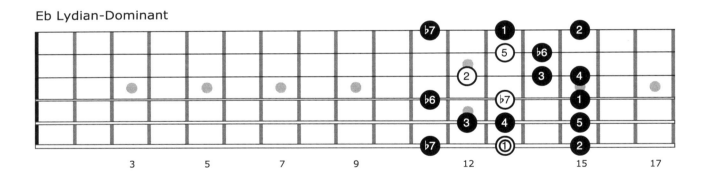

F Mixolydian b6

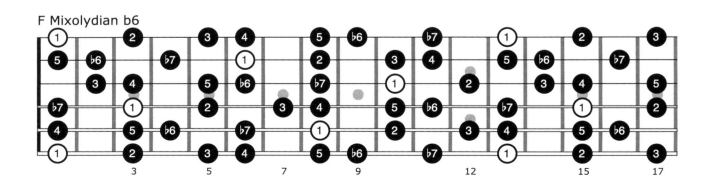

vi. F Locrian ♮2

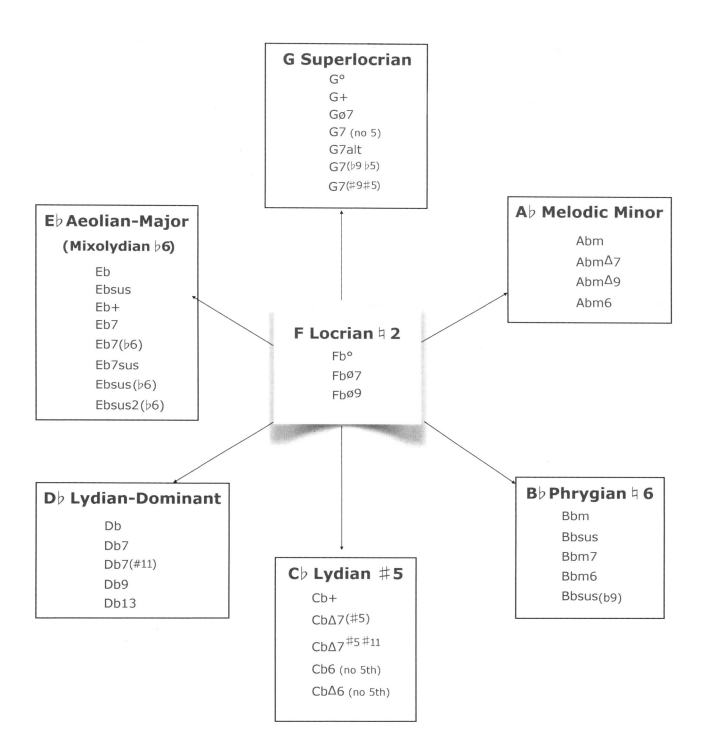

G Superlocrian

G°
G+
Gø7
G7 (no 5)
G7alt
G7(♭9 ♭5)
G7(♯9♯5)

E♭ Aeolian-Major

(Mixolydian ♭6)

Eb
Ebsus
Eb+
Eb7
Eb7(♭6)
Eb7sus
Ebsus(♭6)
Ebsus2(♭6)

A♭ Melodic Minor

Abm
AbmΔ7
AbmΔ9
Abm6

F Locrian ♮2

Fb°
Fbø7
Fbø9

D♭ Lydian-Dominant

Db
Db7
Db7(#11)
Db9
Db13

C♭ Lydian ♯5

Cb+
CbΔ7(♯5)
CbΔ7 ♯5 ♯11
Cb6 (no 5th)
CbΔ6 (no 5th)

B♭ Phrygian ♮6

Bbm
Bbsus
Bbm7
Bbm6
Bbsus(b9)

F Locrian ♮2 - 7 Positions

Fø7

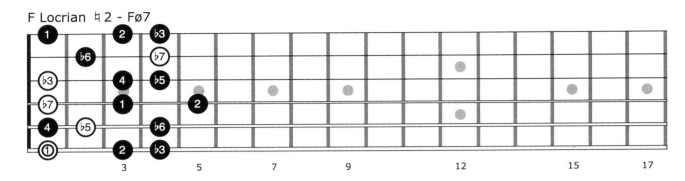

F Locrian ♮2 - Fø7

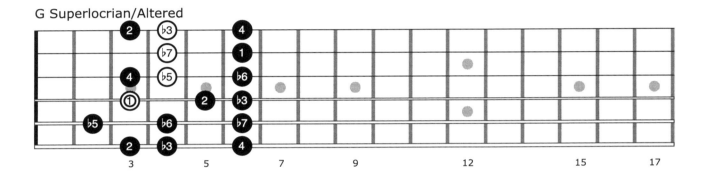

G Superlocrian/Altered

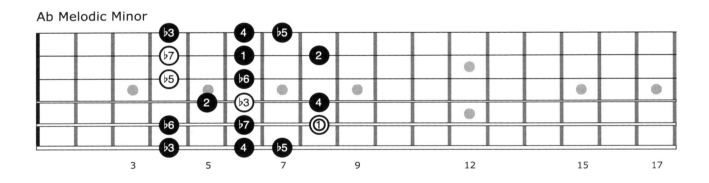

Ab Melodic Minor

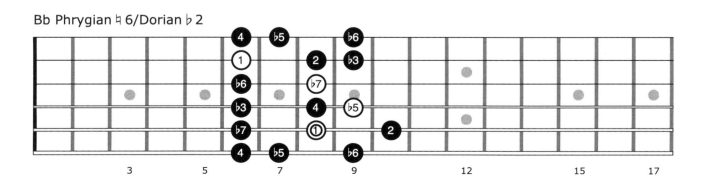

Bb Phrygian ♮6/Dorian ♭2

Cb Lydian-Augmented

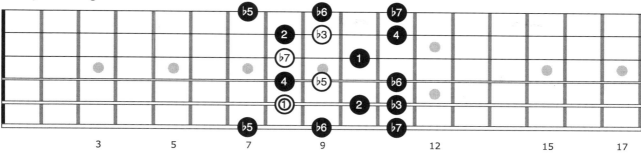

Db Lydian-Dominant

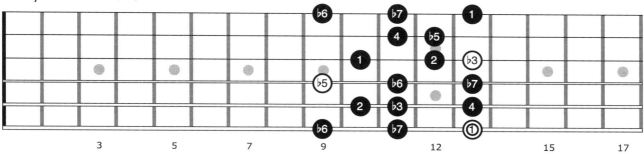

Eb Aeolian-Major/Mixolydian ♭6

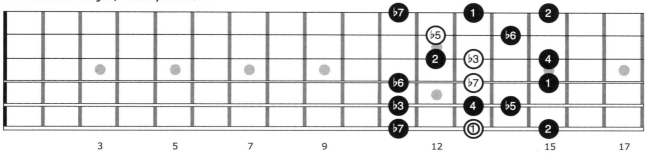

F Locrian ♮2

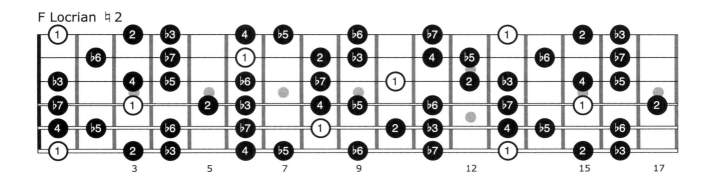

vii. F Superlocrian

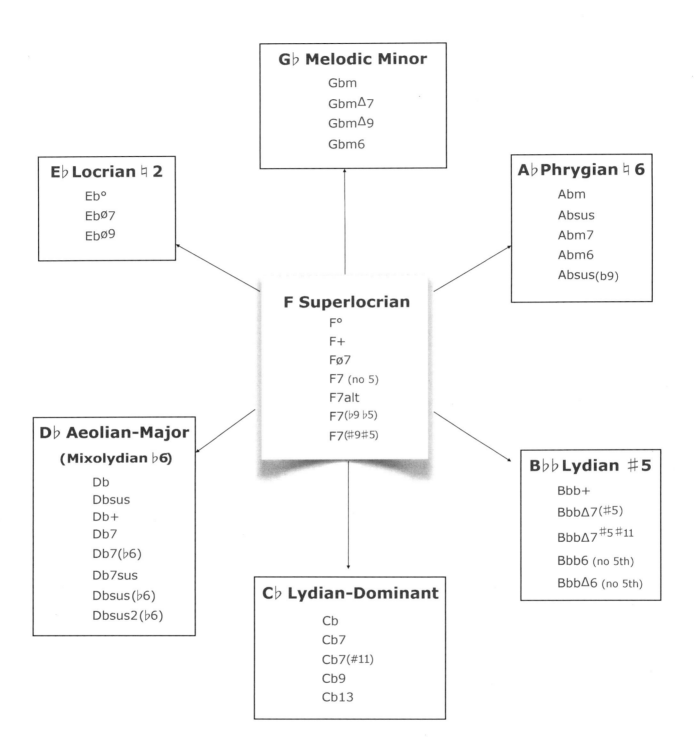

G♭ Melodic Minor

Gbm
Gbm△7
Gbm△9
Gbm6

E♭ Locrian ♮2

Eb°
Ebø7
Ebø9

A♭ Phrygian ♮6

Abm
Absus
Abm7
Abm6
Absus(b9)

F Superlocrian

F°
F+
Fø7
F7 (no 5)
F7alt
F7(♭9 ♭5)
F7(♯9♯5)

D♭ Aeolian-Major

(Mixolydian ♭6)

Db
Dbsus
Db+
Db7
Db7(♭6)
Db7sus
Dbsus(♭6)
Dbsus2(♭6)

C♭ Lydian-Dominant

Cb
Cb7
Cb7(♯11)
Cb9
Cb13

B♭♭ Lydian ♯5

Bbb+
Bbb△7(♯5)
Bbb△7 ♯5 ♯11
Bbb6 (no 5th)
Bbb△6 (no 5th)

F Superlocrian/Altered - 7 Positions   F7

F Superlocrian - G7alt

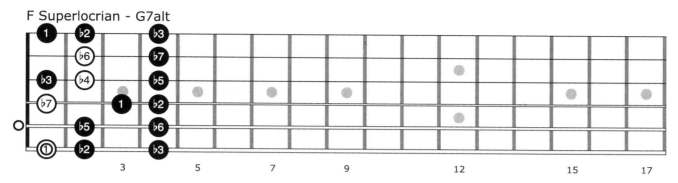

Gb Melodic Minor

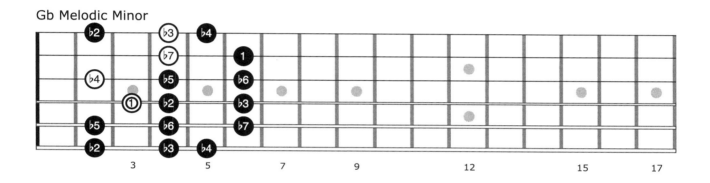

Ab Phrygian ♮6/Dorian ♭2

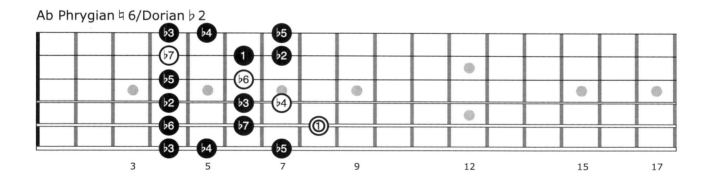

Bbb Lydian-Augmented

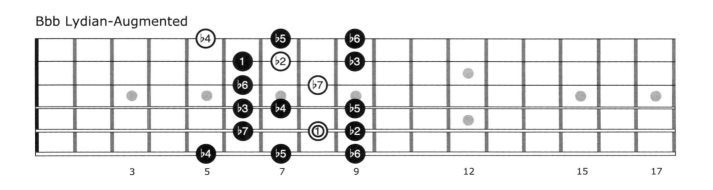

Cb Lydian-Dominant

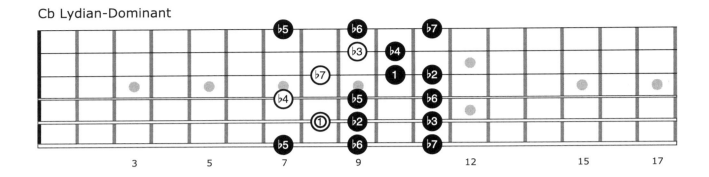

Db Aeolian-Major/Mixolydian ♭6

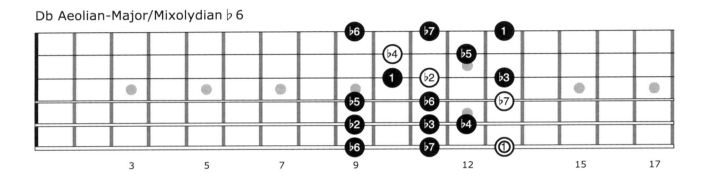

Eb Locrian ♮2

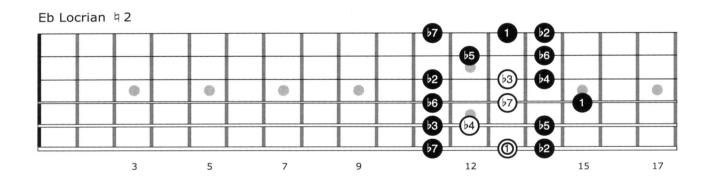

F Superlocrian/Altered

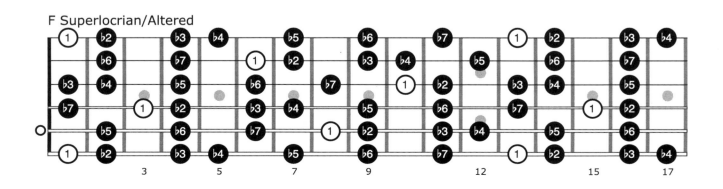

Other Scales

1. Hungarian Minor
(aka Harmonic Minor #4, or Double-Harmonic Minor)
w/ "cool shapes"

2. Harmonic Major
(Ionian b6)
w/ "cool shapes"

(Symmetrical Scales)
3. Whole-Half Diminished
4. Half-Whole Diminished
5. Whole-Tone Scale
6. Augmented Scale

i. A Double Harmonic Minor
(Hungarian Minor, Harmonic Minor #4)

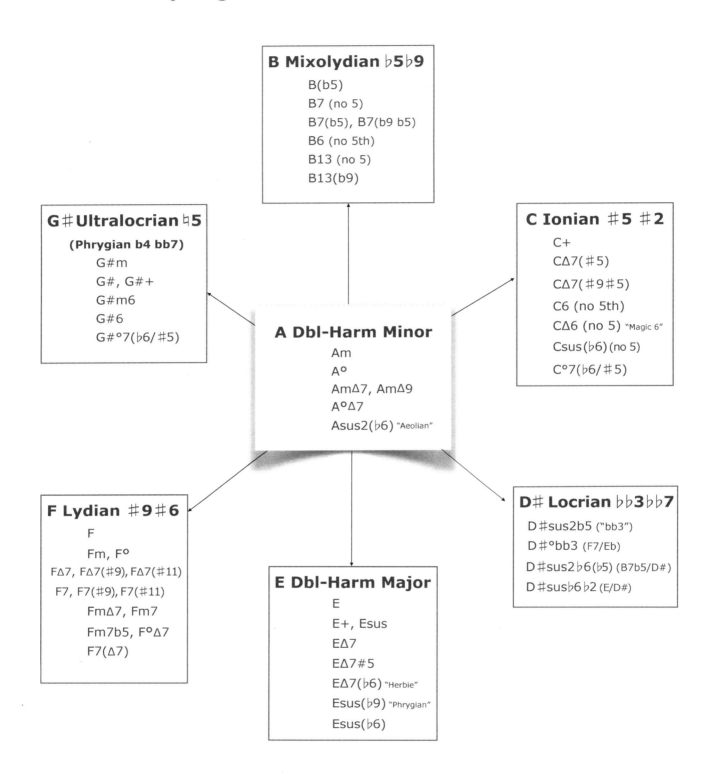

B Mixolydian ♭5♭9

B(b5)
B7 (no 5)
B7(b5), B7(b9 b5)
B6 (no 5th)
B13 (no 5)
B13(b9)

G♯ Ultralocrian ♮5

(Phrygian b4 bb7)
G#m
G#, G#+
G#m6
G#6
G#°7(♭6/♯5)

C Ionian ♯5 ♯2

C+
CΔ7(♯5)
CΔ7(♯9♯5)
C6 (no 5th)
CΔ6 (no 5) "Magic 6"
Csus(♭6)(no 5)
C°7(♭6/♯5)

A Dbl-Harm Minor

Am
A°
AmΔ7, AmΔ9
A°Δ7
Asus2(♭6) "Aeolian"

F Lydian ♯9♯6

F
Fm, F°
FΔ7, FΔ7(♯9), FΔ7(♯11)
F7, F7(♯9), F7(♯11)
FmΔ7, Fm7
Fm7b5, F°Δ7
F7(Δ7)

E Dbl-Harm Major

E
E+, Esus
EΔ7
EΔ7♯5
EΔ7(♭6) "Herbie"
Esus(♭9) "Phrygian"
Esus(♭6)

D♯ Locrian ♭♭3♭♭7

D#sus2b5 ("bb3")
D#°bb3 (F7/Eb)
D#sus2♭6(♭5) (B7b5/D#)
D#sus♭6♭2 (E/D#)

136

(7 modes of) A Double-Harmonic Minor

A Hungarian Minor (Harmonic Minor #4)

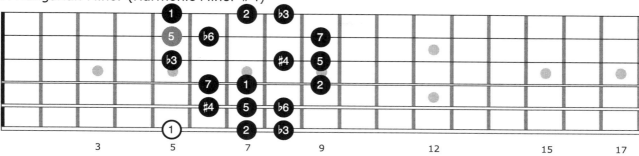

B Oriental (Mixolydian b5 b9)

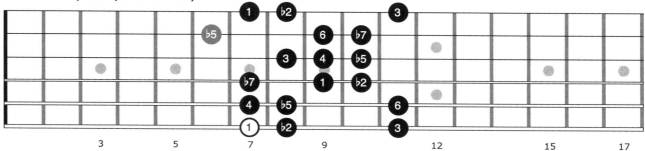

C Ionian Augmented #2

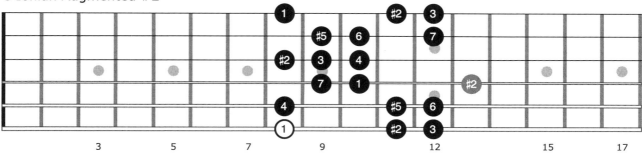

D# Locrian bb3 bb7

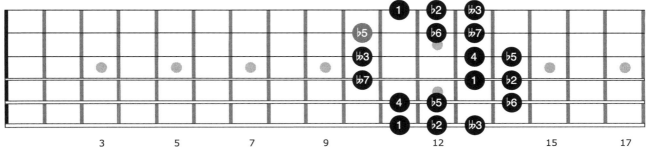

E Double Harmonic Major (Byzantine)

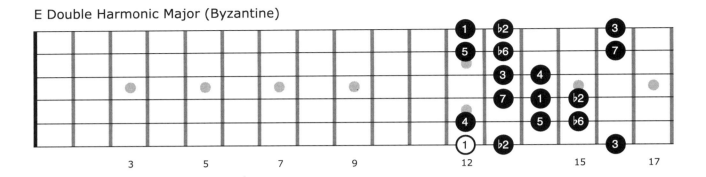

F Lydian #2 #6

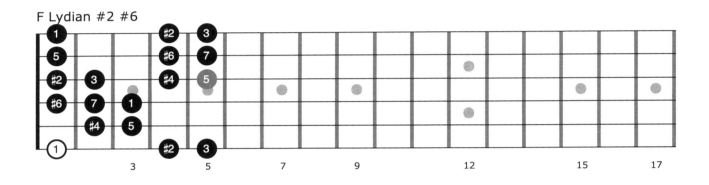

G# Ultraphrygian / Phrygian b4 bb7

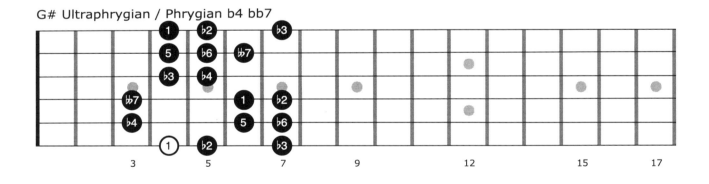

A Hungarian Minor (Harmonic Minor #4)

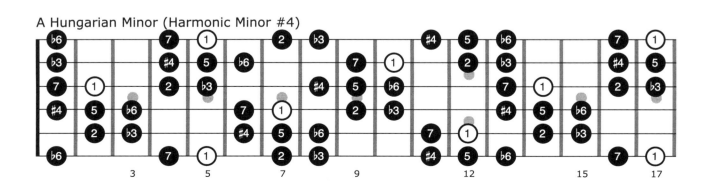

Cool shapes - Hungarian Minor

A Hungarian Minor: Triads up the neck.

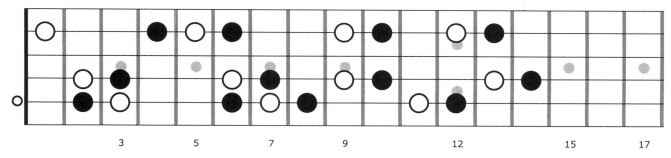

A Hungarian Minor - Quartal 4-7-3, 5-1-4 (etc) shapes up the neck:

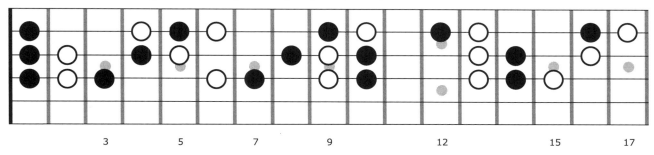

A Hungarian-Minor - 2 different quartal voicings (1-4-7, and 6-2-5) inverted:

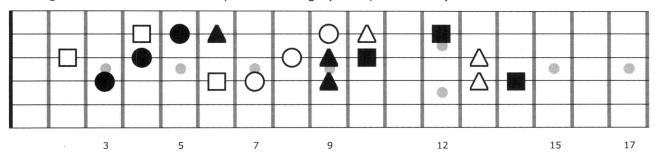

A Hungarian Minor - G#/A & E/F inverted

I. A Harmonic Major

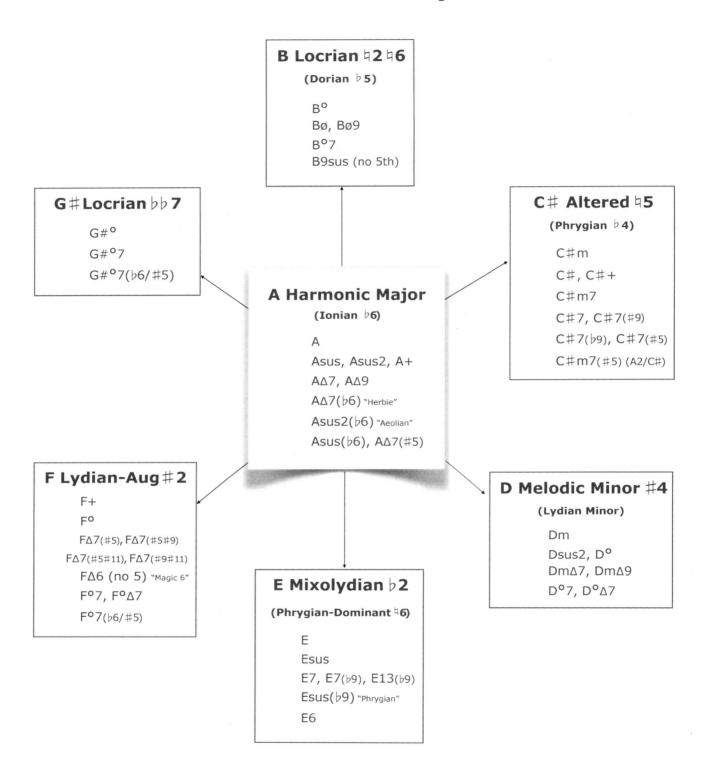

B Locrian ♮2 ♭6

(Dorian ♭5)

B°
Bø, Bø9
B°7
B9sus (no 5th)

G♯ Locrian ♭♭7

G#°
G#°7
G#°7(♭6/#5)

C♯ Altered ♮5

(Phrygian ♭4)

C#m
C#, C#+
C#m7
C#7, C#7(#9)
C#7(♭9), C#7(#5)
C#m7(#5) (A2/C#)

A Harmonic Major

(Ionian ♭6)

A
Asus, Asus2, A+
AΔ7, AΔ9
AΔ7(♭6) "Herbie"
Asus2(♭6) "Aeolian"
Asus(♭6), AΔ7(#5)

F Lydian-Aug ♯2

F+
F°
FΔ7(#5), FΔ7(#5#9)
FΔ7(#5#11), FΔ7(#9#11)
FΔ6 (no 5) "Magic 6"
F°7, F°Δ7
F°7(♭6/#5)

D Melodic Minor ♯4

(Lydian Minor)

Dm
Dsus2, D°
DmΔ7, DmΔ9
D°7, D°Δ7

E Mixolydian ♭2

(Phrygian-Dominant ♮6)

E
Esus
E7, E7(♭9), E13(♭9)
Esus(♭9) "Phrygian"
E6

(7 modes of) A Harmonic Major

A Harmonic-Major (Ionian b6, Aeolian-Major Δ7)

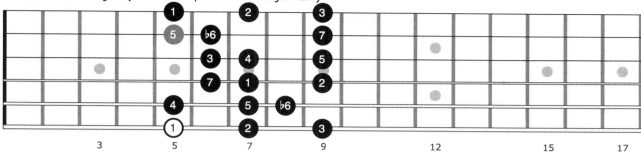

B Locrian ♮2 ♮6 (Dorian b5)

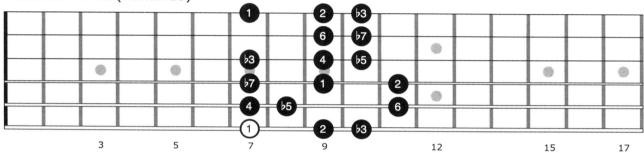

C# Altered ♮5 (Phrygian b4)

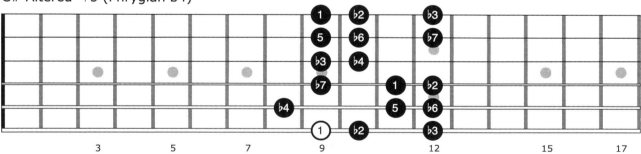

D Lydian-Minor (Melodic Minor #4)

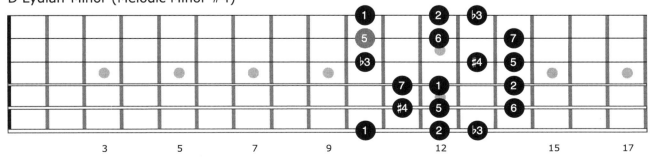

E Mixolydian b2 (Phrygian-Dominant ♮6)

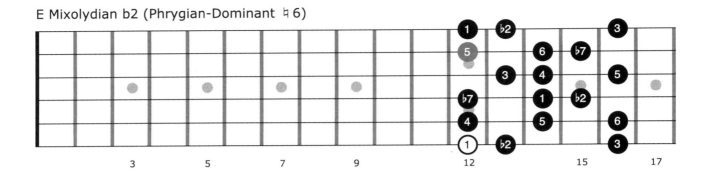

F Lydian-Augmented #2

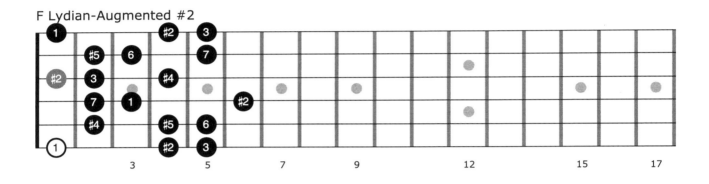

G# Locrian bb7

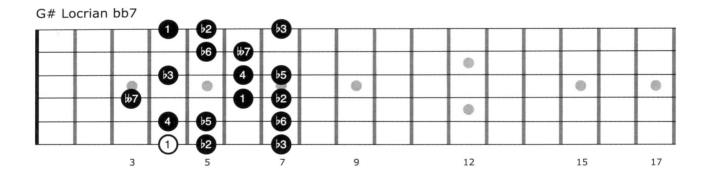

A Harmonic Major (Ionian b6)

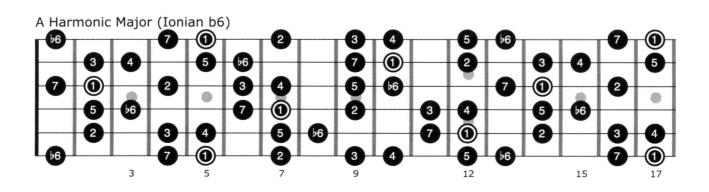

Cool shapes - Harmonic Major

A Harmonic-Major: Triads up the neck.

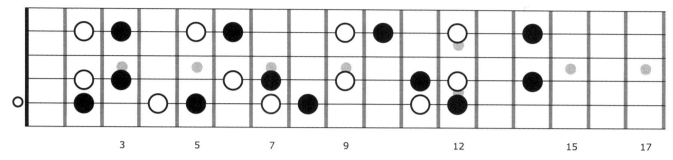

A Harmonic Major - Quartal 4-7-3, 5-1-4 (etc) shapes up the neck:

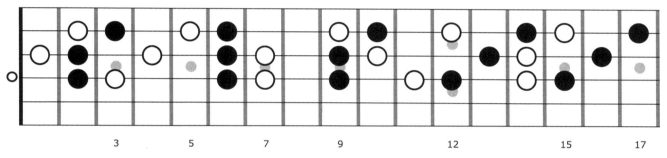

A Harmonic-Major - 2 different quartal voicings (4-7-3, and 6-2-5) inverted:

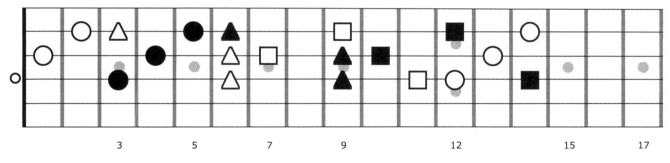

A Harmonic Major - C#/D & E/F inverted:

Whole-1/2 Diminished Scale

1 - 2 - ♭3 - 4 - ♭5 - #5 - 6 - 7

C - D - D#/E♭ - F - F#/G♭ - G#/A♭ - A - B

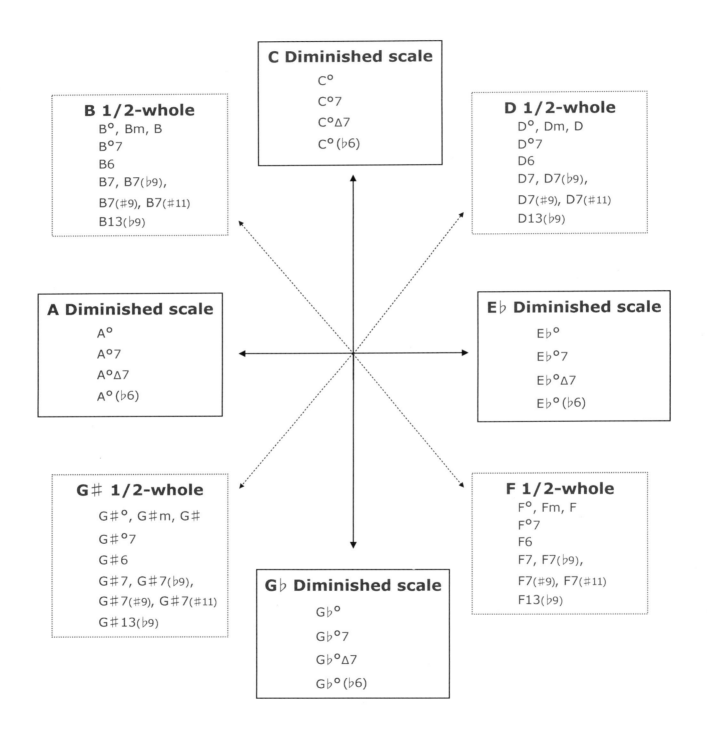

C Diminished scale
C°
C°7
C°Δ7
C° (♭6)

B 1/2-whole
B°, Bm, B
B°7
B6
B7, B7(♭9),
B7(#9), B7(#11)
B13(♭9)

D 1/2-whole
D°, Dm, D
D°7
D6
D7, D7(♭9),
D7(#9), D7(#11)
D13(♭9)

A Diminished scale
A°
A°7
A°Δ7
A° (♭6)

E♭ Diminished scale
E♭°
E♭°7
E♭°Δ7
E♭° (♭6)

G# 1/2-whole
G#°, G#m, G#
G#°7
G#6
G#7, G#7(♭9),
G#7(#9), G#7(#11)
G#13(♭9)

F 1/2-whole
F°, Fm, F
F°7
F6
F7, F7(♭9),
F7(#9), F7(#11)
F13(♭9)

G♭ Diminished scale
G♭°
G♭°7
G♭°Δ7
G♭° (♭6)

Whole-Half Diminished Scale - Various shapes

C°7, C°Δ7

C Diminished (Whole Half)

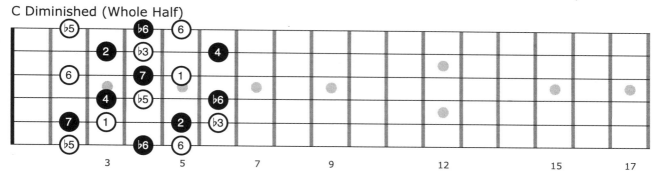

C Diminished (Whole Half)

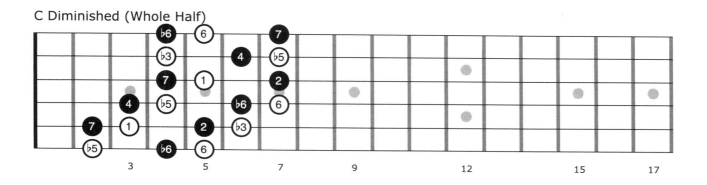

C Diminished (Whole Half)

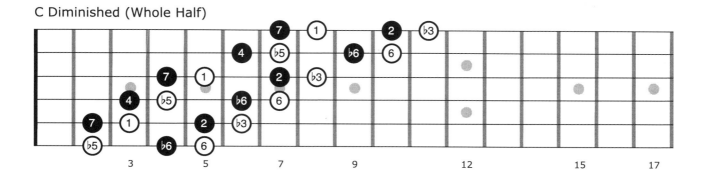

C Diminished (Whole Half)

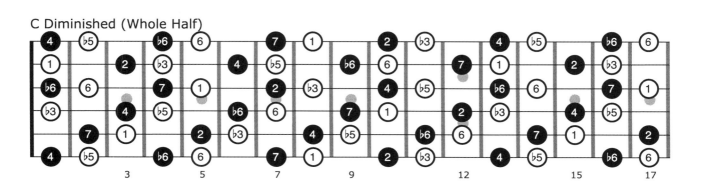

1/2-Whole Diminished Scale

1 - ♭2 - #2 - 3 - #4 - 5 - 6 - ♭7

D - D#/E♭ - F - F#/G♭ - G#/A♭ - A - B - C

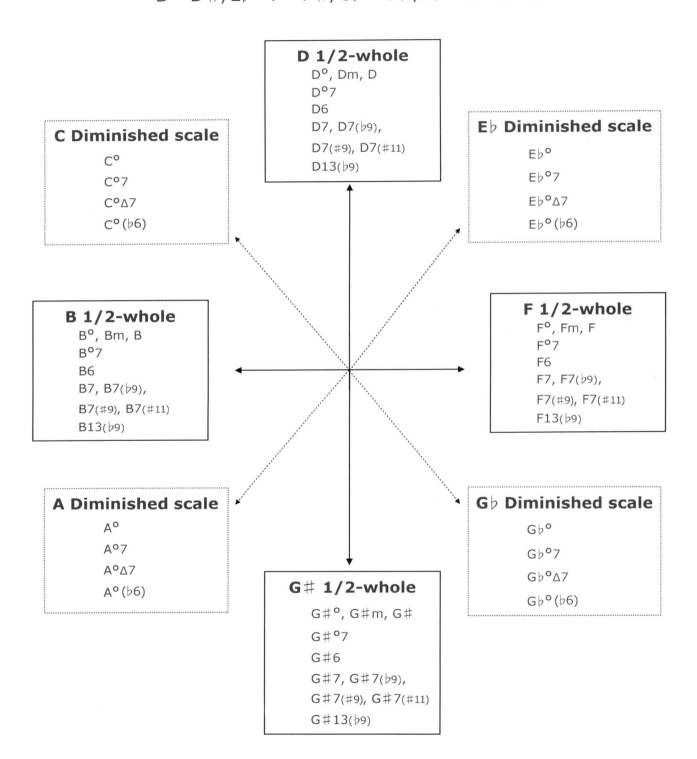

D 1/2-whole
D°, Dm, D
D°7
D6
D7, D7(♭9),
D7(#9), D7(#11)
D13(♭9)

E♭ Diminished scale
E♭°
E♭°7
E♭°△7
E♭°(♭6)

C Diminished scale
C°
C°7
C°△7
C°(♭6)

B 1/2-whole
B°, Bm, B
B°7
B6
B7, B7(♭9),
B7(#9), B7(#11)
B13(♭9)

F 1/2-whole
F°, Fm, F
F°7
F6
F7, F7(♭9),
F7(#9), F7(#11)
F13(♭9)

A Diminished scale
A°
A°7
A°△7
A°(♭6)

G♭ Diminished scale
G♭°
G♭°7
G♭°△7
G♭°(♭6)

G# 1/2-whole
G#°, G#m, G#
G#°7
G#6
G#7, G#7(♭9),
G#7(#9), G#7(#11)
G#13(♭9)

Half-Whole Diminished Scale - Various shapes

D7, D13(b9),
D7#11#9

D Diminished (Half Whole)

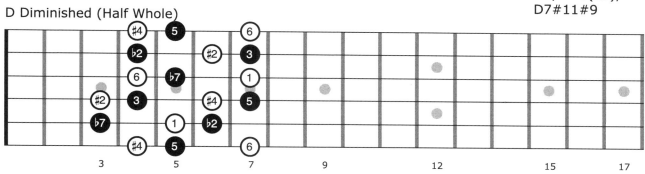

D Diminished (Half Whole)

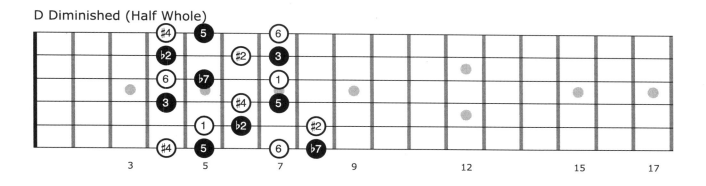

D Diminished (Half Whole)

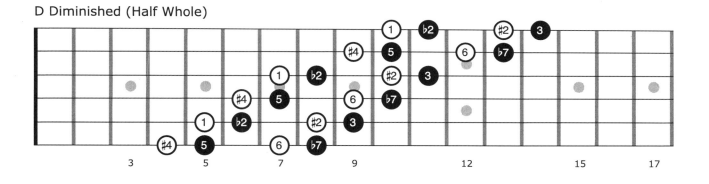

D Diminished (Half Whole)

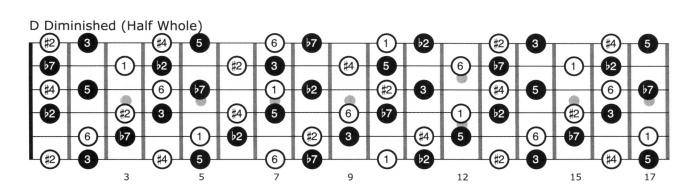

147

Whole-Tone Scale

1 - 2 - 3 - #4 - #5 - #6 (♭7)

G - A - B - C# - D# - E# (F)

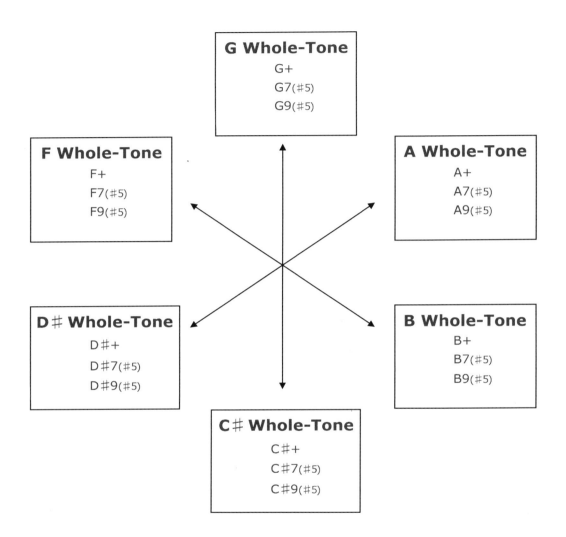

G Whole-Tone
G+
G7(#5)
G9(#5)

A Whole-Tone
A+
A7(#5)
A9(#5)

F Whole-Tone
F+
F7(#5)
F9(#5)

B Whole-Tone
B+
B7(#5)
B9(#5)

D# Whole-Tone
D#+
D#7(#5)
D#9(#5)

C# Whole-Tone
C#+
C#7(#5)
C#9(#5)

Whole Tone Scale - Various shapes

G+, G7#5, G9#5

G Whole Tone

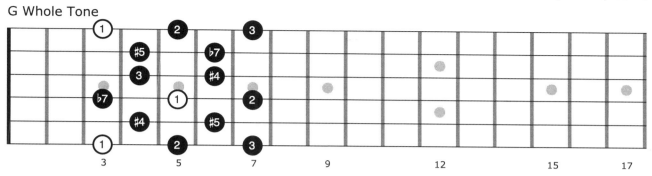

G Whole Tone

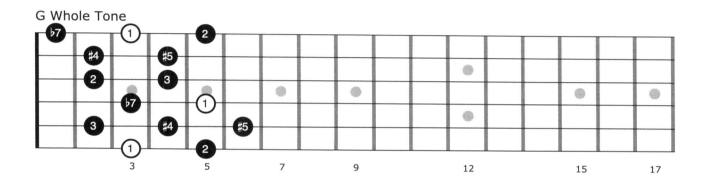

G Whole Tone

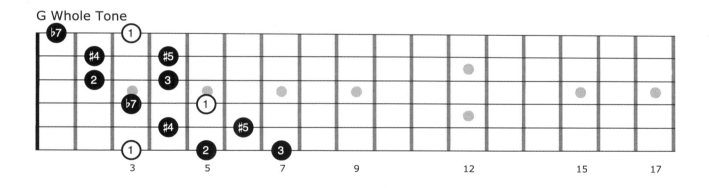

G Whole Tone

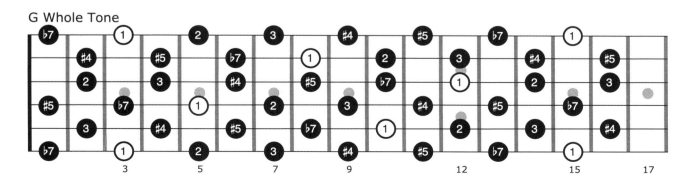

A Augmented Scale
(A - C - C♯/D♭ - E - F - G♯)

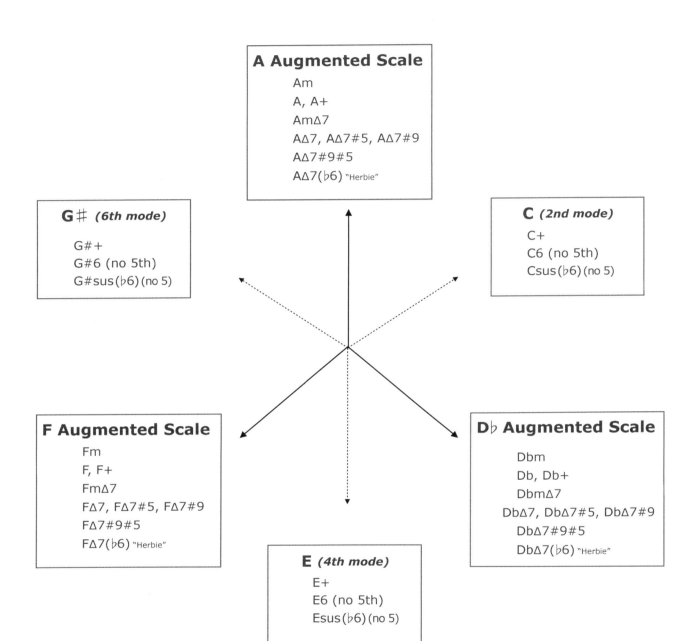

A Augmented Scale

Am

A, A+

AmΔ7

AΔ7, AΔ7#5, AΔ7#9

AΔ7#9#5

AΔ7(♭6) "Herbie"

G♯ *(6th mode)*

G#+

G#6 (no 5th)

G#sus(♭6)(no 5)

C *(2nd mode)*

C+

C6 (no 5th)

Csus(♭6)(no 5)

F Augmented Scale

Fm

F, F+

FmΔ7

FΔ7, FΔ7#5, FΔ7#9

FΔ7#9#5

FΔ7(♭6) "Herbie"

D♭ Augmented Scale

Dbm

Db, Db+

DbmΔ7

DbΔ7, DbΔ7#5, DbΔ7#9

DbΔ7#9#5

DbΔ7(♭6) "Herbie"

E *(4th mode)*

E+

E6 (no 5th)

Esus(♭6)(no 5)

Augmented Scale - Various shapes

Am, A, A+
AmΔ7, AΔ7, AΔ7#5

A Augmented

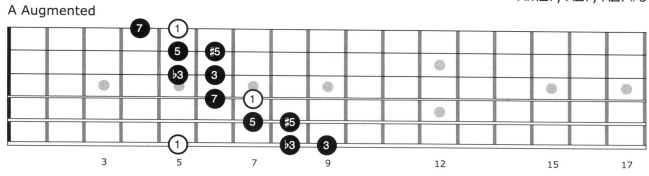

A Augmented

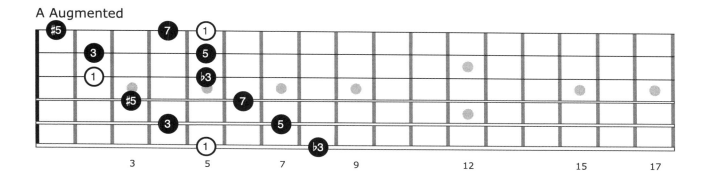

A Augmented (Finger numbers)

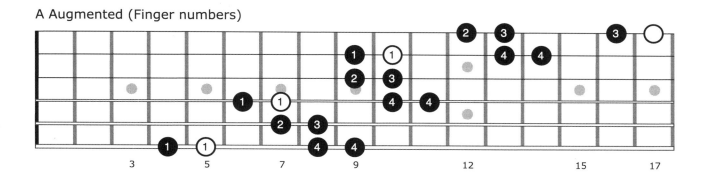

A Augmented

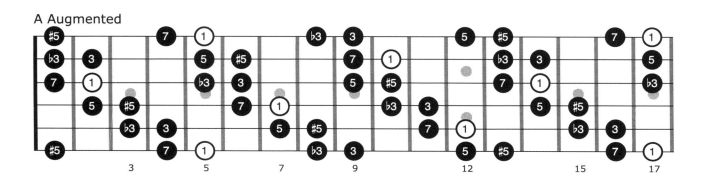

Notes

Notes